Fighting Tradition

**Asian and Pacific American
Transcultural Studies**

Russell C. Leong
General Editor

Fighting Tradition

A Marine's Journey to Justice

CAPTAIN BRUCE I. YAMASHITA, USMCR

University of Hawai'i Press
Honolulu

In Association with
UCLA Asian American Studies Center
Los Angeles

To Mother and Pop

© 2003 University of Hawai'i Press
All rights reserved

Printed in the United States of America
08 07 06 05 04 03   6 5 4 3 2 1

Library of Congress Cataloging-in-Publication Data

Yamashita, Bruce I.
    Fighting tradition : a marine's journey to justice / Bruce I.
    Yamashita.
        p. cm.
    Includes index.
    ISBN 0–8248–2410–5 (cloth : alk. paper) —
    ISBN 0–8248–2745–7 (paper : alk. paper)
    1. Yamashita, Bruce I.—Trials, litigation, etc. 2. United
States. Marine Corps—Officers—Biography. 3. United States.
Marine Corps—Lawyers—Biography. 4. Race discrimination—
United States—Case studies. 5. United States. Marine Corps—
Minorities. 6. Japanese Americans—Civil rights—Case studies.
I. Title.

VE25.Y36A3 2003
356.9'6089'956073—dc21
[B]

                                                    2003043446

University of Hawai'i Press books are printed on acid-free
paper and meet the guidelines for permanence and
durability of the Council on Library Resources.

Designed by Bookcomp, Inc.

Printed by The Maple-Vail Book Manufacturing Group

Contents

Prologue

Rarely do I have the luxury of a midweek afternoon walk through my Dupont Circle neighborhood, but my morning meetings with clients had been canceled, and D.C. Superior Court, where I thought I'd have to be, was closed. I couldn't take any more of the same scenes on CNN, being repeated over and over again. With an F-16 fighter jet patrolling the empty skies in the distance, I forced myself out of the Boston House into the sunlight of a beautiful September day.

Out on the street, I was struck by an unusual quiet and an unfamiliar sight. American flags adorned buildings. They flew from makeshift flag poles, and were draped in shop windows. Homemade paper flags were pasted on doors. It was a display of patriotism for a nation in crisis on September 12, 2001. I walked through the neighborhood, and let the sights and quiet of the deserted streets wash over me. Like every American, I was in shock over the tragedy of the day before. Like everyone else, I needed to cling to something in a world seemingly gone mad. For many of us, it was the flag, a tangible symbol of our great and powerful country and a reminder that we would respond. But with a perspective unlike most others, I couldn't help but ponder the deeper meaning behind this red, white, and blue landscape.

It seemed that as each flag was raised, draped, or pasted, each of us became compelled to join in. To not show the flag meant that we were unpatriotic. To stand for America, we were required to conform, no questions asked. From the White House, the president's press secretary had warned us to watch what we said in the moment of crisis. Even months after the attack, a member of Congress who voted against emergency legislation would be accused of being un-American. Groups that defended civil liberties would be attacked as soft on terrorism. Those who questioned military action would be labeled as traitors.

I couldn't help but wonder how ironic this was for a nation that is greater because of individual Americans who stood on principle. I couldn't help but wonder how a nation that acknowledged the unconstitutionality of the internment of American citizens because of their race could subject a new group to harassment merely because they looked like the terrorist enemies of America. I couldn't help but wonder how patriotism could be used to justify expediency over due process, and require only the flying of a flag absent the values of freedom, justice, and courage.

As I headed back to the Boston House, I knew that in the ensuing months and years, America's greatness would be measured not only by its valor on the battlefield, but also by its vigilance in remaining true to its ideals. My thoughts and the quiet of the deserted streets were interrupted by a car with the driver honking his horn, and both passengers leaning out of their windows chanting "U.S.A.!" A part of me wanted to join in and shout "Urah!" But instead, moved by the seriousness of the moment, all I could muster was a faint smile. As I gazed into the distance, I could see a younger man beginning to learn that patriotism isn't just what he displayed on the outside, but also, when times were loneliest, what he could summon from within.

Acknowledgments

THE SUPPORT OF DON NAKANISHI, CHAIRMAN OF THE UCLA Asian American Studies Center, and Russell Leong, editor of the series Intersections, revived an all but abandoned project. Steve Okino provided critical assistance in rewriting the original manuscript, and from the beginning allowed himself to be my sounding board. My editors, Sharon Yamamoto and Masako Ikeda, brought to the project enthusiasm, insight, and professional expertise. To these individuals, I extend my heartfelt appreciation.

This book would not have been possible without the countless individuals: some named, many nameless, who wrote letters of support, attended fundraisers and press conferences, volunteered their services, and offered words of inspiration. You know who you are. I owe you a debt of gratitude that I can never repay. This book belongs to you.

Introduction

HAD I BEEN THINKING CLEARLY, I WOULD HAVE known what was coming, but the ten most difficult weeks of my life had taken their toll. I was beat up physically and emotionally. And I was not alone. That's what Marine Corps Officer Candidate School (OCS) did to people.

Still, I was dead set on being a Marine officer. Graduation was four days away, and I thought the worst was over. Despite the hellish weeks at OCS, I had survived. I was convinced I had shown I had the right stuff to make it.

The problem was that the Marine Corps didn't agree. It took years for me to learn that the decision had little to do with how I performed. Though no one would admit it at the time, the decision was based largely on who I was. It was made quickly, perhaps on the first day of OCS, and there was nothing I could do to change it. The officers in charge made sure of that; the racial epithets that the staff screamed at me almost every day sealed my fate:

"Kamikaze man!"

"Go back to your own country!"

"During World War II, we whipped your Japanese ass!"

Now, the screaming was over. The damage had been done. I had never in thirty-three years of life ever encountered the racial venom hurled at me at Officer Candidate School in Quantico, Virginia. Never in Hawaii, known for its rainbow of people, cultures, and ethnicities. Never in Japan, where at least I looked like I fit in, even if I didn't.

Never at Georgetown Law School, where, if there was racial hostility, none was directed at me. I had no understanding of how racial harassment could spiral beyond mere words, of how it poisons minds, of how it dooms its targets to failure, especially when the harassers hold the power.

2

As a third-generation American whose grandparents had emigrated from Japan, I was fair game for these old-line Marines. At OCS, they played the race card early and often. They had a harmless-sounding euphemism for it: "controlled stress." The Marine Corps claimed such harassment toughened up their officer candidates. Later, I would discover how it turned my classmates against me, and tainted the official record, especially with regard to the subjective "leadership" evaluation. Most important, I would secure Marine Corps statistics showing that the OCS command had routinely kicked out minorities at higher rates than whites. What I did with those statistics, and the facts on which they were based, would turn the Corps inside out over the way it treated minorities and women.

But I didn't know any of that on April 7, 1989. All I knew, or wanted to believe, was that the racial harassment and unfair treatment had been a test of my mettle. It was the only explanation I could muster for the bizarre conduct of the OCS staff. The cruel reality was that it had not been a test at all, but a done deal from the beginning, and I was facing the inevitable slash of the executioner's ax. And waiting with me were the four other minority candidates in my platoon. This wasn't going to be a routine review.

It was called the final review board, and it had the power to recommend that a candidate graduate or be kicked out. The board had made its decision long ago, and now was prepared to finish the job.

Ordered into the office of the commanding officer (CO), I gathered myself for one final try at persuading them that

I had the mettle to be a Marine. I stood straight, looking as much like a recruiting poster as I could:

"Candidate Yamashita reporting as ordered, Sir!"

I had never been in this office before, and I risked shifting my eyes to take it all in. Certificates, awards, and diplomas covered the walls; the commanding officer, Colonel C.W. Reinke, was anchored behind a huge desk, flanked by the flags of the United States, the Corps, and Officer Candidate School. I rarely saw him during training, and the sight of him now, surrounded by all these trappings of power, was frightening.

The rest of the top brass was there, too: Major Winter, the company commander; Captain Mortenson, the executive officer; and Lieutenant Eshelman, my platoon commander. The only new face was Captain Garcia, the battalion executive officer. All seated, staring at me, their eyes expressionless.

Eshelman began to read a statement. "This candidate is still behind the power curve. I strongly recommend disenrollment."

How can he say that? I wondered. He's the one who let the harassment go on, let it spin out of control, and did nothing to stop it.

He went on with his case against me. Evaluations were unsatisfactory, he said. Leadership qualities were lacking.

It would take years for the Marines to admit that there were problems with those evaluations. It would take years for the Corps to acknowledge that there had been a pattern of discrimination against minorities. It would take years for justice to be done. But on this day, I knew none of these things.

Colonel Reinke asked if I had anything to say for myself.

I straightened up and proffered the only defense I had at the time. "To disenroll me now would be a mistake. I have made great progress, and . . ."

He cut me off with the slam of his gavel. "Candidate Yamashita, you are DISENROLLED."

I can't remember if I reacted. I do remember feeling like my life had ended, that my future was down the drain. I know at OCS they try to break you down in the guise of toughening you up. Regardless of how broken I felt right then, I was not going to give them the satisfaction of knowing they had succeeded.

"Aye, aye, Sir!" I yelled.

I wheeled about and started marching out.

"Candidate Yamashita," Colonel Reinke shouted. I froze.

"I heard you flunked your bar exam," he called out mockingly. The other officers broke out in laughter.

They had done everything they could over nine weeks to make me quit. When I didn't go along with their program, they had to kick me out. It was good for a laugh then, a little celebration perhaps for preserving the unwritten, lily-white tradition of the Corps.

Defeated and confused, I returned home to Hawaii. With no job and no prospects, I passed the time brooding over my fate. I had wanted to serve my country, and I had expected a fair chance to try. My questions were the same ones that everyone asks when they fail: "Why me? Why now?"

Family and friends told me to move on with my life. But I couldn't let go of my experience at Officer Candidate School. It had shaken my belief in the system, which was the most important thing that my parents had instilled in me. In law school, I thought all those ethnic minority, women, and gay students who were clamoring for equal rights were wimps and whiners who should just learn to relax. But after coming face to face with the discrimination they had talked about, I was angry. All those boycotts and marches that I heard about during the 1960s and 1970s weren't just interesting events. They sprang from pain and humiliation—the same sort of pain and humiliation that I was feeling now. To accept what had happened to me would be cowardly.

My decision would take me on a journey of self-discovery. I began to see what for years I had chosen to ignore: that discrimination was a real, pervasive, and insidious part of American society. I began to understand the meaning of courage, unselfishness, and unwavering commitment to principle. I began to appreciate a new sense of duty to country, which would make me a better American.

Now, as I wear the bars that signify my standing as an officer in the United States Marine Corps, I sometimes recall the faces of those at OCS years ago. I hear their laughter, feel their mockery, and remember wondering: What kind of leaders humiliate rather than elevate, destroy rather than build? How many young people had they devastated through their crazy concepts of leadership? If that was Marine policy, wasn't that policy wrong?

It took years to uncover the answers. But first, someone had to ask the questions.

1

"A Clear Demonstration of Patriotism and Loyalty"

February 6, 1989

Monday morning, 6 a.m. The radio alarm blared. I was at the Boston House, a condominium in the Dupont Circle neighborhood of Washington, D.C. My first impulse was to roll over, turn it off, and go back to sleep. But today was the day. February 6, 1989, the start of the 140th Marine Corps Officer Candidate School at Quantico, Virginia. I was ready.

At the foot of the bed was a small traveling bag. Next to it was a copy of "As an Officer of Marines," a colorful recruitment brochure: . . . *OCS is make or break. Go or no go. It's weeks of some of the toughest physical training in the world. It's where you . . . and we . . . find out if you've got what it takes to be an officer of Marines.* I carried it wherever I went, and had read it over and over again.

The Marine Corps had sent me instructions. There was a list of items I would need to bring: wire hangers, travel iron, Q-tips, black pens, nail clippers, rags, and skivvies. There was even an imperative for attire: "You must dress better than the average citizen . . . even off base you will be seen and must be squared away." With this in mind, I had laid out my outfit the night before: sport shirt, slacks with a belt, dark socks, leather shoes, and a jacket.

I rolled out of bed, took what I would later consider a

luxury—a long, hot shower—and dressed. Sipping cappuccino, I scanned the morning edition of the *Washington Post*. I didn't expect to be back until after ten weeks of Officer Candidate School, so I went around checking to see that the electricity and gas were turned off. I locked the door behind me; as I left the elevator, I waved to the front desk clerk, a recent immigrant from Ghana.

"So, you're finally off to become a Marine," he grinned.

"Yeah, I'm outta here," I answered, rushing through the lobby.

He gave me a thumbs-up sign. When I opened the door, the raw winter air hit my face, at first refreshing, but soon numbing. There were patches of snow on the ground. Graduate students were walking to their classes at Johns Hopkins School of Advanced International Studies nearby. Office workers were making their way into the National Cable Television Association building across the street. It reminded me that I was leaving the creature comforts of the civilian world.

I stepped out and hailed a cab on Massachusetts Avenue. As we drove off, passing the Peruvian Embassy on the left and the Brookings Institute on the right, I recalled the words on the OCS Certificate of Acceptance: VOLUNTARY MEMBERSHIP IN THIS ELITE MILITARY ORGANIZATION IS A CLEAR DEMONSTRATION OF PATRIOTISM AND LOYALTY.

I reported to the Hyattsville, Maryland, Marine Corps recruiting station, along with seven others from the Washington area.

"Becoming an officer of Marines should not be taken lightly. You will have unquestioned authority, but also complete responsibility and accountability for whatever happens on your watch," lectured Captain Neil Rodenbeck, officer selection officer (OSO).

Despite some earlier difficulties with Captain Rodenbeck, his office had been helpful in arranging initial transportation from Hawaii to the Washington area, and that day he treated me no differently than anyone else. Most of the others looked as though they had walked off a Marine poster. But we shared one thing in common: we wanted to be officers of Marines. We had been picked via a rigorous selection process: physical fitness tests, medical examinations, academic requirements, background checks, and recommendations. We left the recruiting station in a van headed toward Washington National Airport, where we would join candidates flying in from around the country.

We arrived at the airport and were whisked to the second floor, where other candidates were waiting. There were now forty of us. We had come from all over the country and from different walks of life. The excitement turned to apprehension.

"OCS is about getting up at 0500 when you're dead tired and your bones rattle. It is about teamwork, hustle, dedication," lectured Captain Rodenbeck. He continued to impress upon us the heavy responsibility of being an officer before he turned and disappeared.

For a few moments we were on our own. One of the candidates was part of the Enlisted Commissioning Program, an ECP; he had been selected to attend OCS from the enlisted ranks, after attaining the rank of sergeant. There would be seven ECPs at the 140th OCS; the rest of us would look to them for guidance. Nervously, we exchanged pleasantries. As others continued to talk, I recalled the events leading up to OCS.

During my final year of law school, I had to decide what I was going to do with the rest of my life. Classmates who were military officers planted the idea of doing a tour with the military. After being cooped up in a classroom, I liked the thought of being both a lawyer and an officer. I had nothing against entering a law firm, but as I saw it, that could come later. I applied for the U.S. Army Judge Advocate General (JAG) Corps and was accepted. But before making a commitment, I wanted to explore the other branches.

Life is filled with ironic twists and turns. By chance at one of the recruiting stations I had visited, I briefly met Major Harvey Hopson, a black officer. He was friendly and encouraged me to consider the Marines. He even took the time to put me in touch with Major Ernest Kimoto, a judge advocate, stationed at Camp Smith in Hawaii.

On a trip home, I had made arrangements to meet Major Kimoto. He was waiting for me in the parking lot, wearing a camouflage uniform. He was short and muscular, and reminded me of a bull terrier. We shook hands and although his posture and bearing exuded "rough, tough, Marine," I sensed a gentleness of spirit. Major Kimoto had been born and raised in Hawaii, and had enlisted in 1968 at the height of the Vietnam War.

I followed him into his office. It was strictly utilitarian, a far cry from the plush law offices in Washington, D.C., and New York. Major Kimoto felt that my background would serve the Marine Corps well. I was impressed by the fact that, unlike other branches of the military, the Marine Corps required all officers, including lawyers, to complete Officer Candidate School. Days later, his parting words still echoed in my ears:

"Lawyers in the other branches go through a two-week charm course, but in the Marine Corps you earn your bars. In the Marine Corps you are an officer first, and a lawyer second."

I was hooked.

At the Hyattsville recruiting station, I met with Captain Neil Rodenbeck, an OSO. Rodenbeck informed me that it was a race against the clock, for I would have to pass a bar and graduate from the next Officer Candidate School by my 33rd birthday, a year away. He advised me to take the Hawaii bar because the results would come out months earlier than other state bars. I packed up and raced home to Hawaii. A week before the exam, Rodenbeck called to inform me that even if I passed, the paperwork could not be completed by the start of the next OCS, and therefore, I was ineligible to join the Marine Corps.

I had felt, at best, poorly advised. To add insult to injury, I later learned that I had flunked the bar exam. My father, who saw the exam as the final challenge in my educational career, tried to hide his disappointment, which made me feel even worse.

"Well, I guess you just do it again," was my mother's response. Her typical "if you tried your best, angels can do no better" attitude helped me to look forward, rather than wallow in self-pity.

After years of school, I had nothing to show. After speaking with Major Kimoto about what I should do, I wrote to Hawaii Senator Daniel K. Inouye, chairman of the Defense Appropriations Subcommittee, explaining my situation. Inouye was a household word in Hawaii, and a source of pride for the Japanese American community. He was a decorated member of the 442nd Regimental Combat Team (RCT) in World War II, and in the 1950s helped to topple Hawaii's ruling Republican Party, which had presided over a power structure closed to people of color. Inouye had been a member of the Senate Watergate Committee, whose hearings ultimately forced the resignation of President Richard Nixon. He had done much for the people of Hawaii. With the senator involved, the issue was quickly resolved. I got an age waiver, and submitted my application as a ground candidate with the understanding that I would be transferred to a law contract once I passed the bar. A few weeks later my application was approved, and I was accepted into the 140th OCS.

While getting approval from the Marine Corps had been difficult, getting it from family and friends had proven to be even tougher. After my meeting with Major Kimoto, I had tested the waters by mentioning it to my sister, Margaret, on the phone. We had always been close. She was the oldest and I was the youngest of four siblings. Five years my senior, she had always watched out for me. She was an idealist, and tended to wear her heart on her sleeve. Because she was a product of the 1960s, I could have predicted her response.

"Are you nuts!? Everybody tries to stay out of the military, not enlist! And why the Marine Corps?"

I explained my reasons, which calmed her down a bit.

"Well, then join the Air Force; at least they have some class!" she responded.

Disgusted, I told her, "Let's change the subject . . . heck, I still have to be accepted."

"Let's pray they don't take you." she said.

I gave up. "Break it to Mother and Pop, okay?"

Margaret said later that my parents' reaction wasn't any better. My father just shook his head.

"Does he want to give your father a heart attack!" my mother exclaimed.

They felt that I would be happier joining a law firm. Moreover, they saw the Corps as a bunch of rednecks with guns. But that worn-out stereotype had angered me. My mind was made up. I passionately defended my decision and the Corps.

2

"Exactly What I Had Expected"

"Hey, you! Stand up and get in line!" a harsh voice jolted me out of my reverie. A young Marine corporal stood over me. Passengers and ticketing agents looked up to see what was causing the commotion. We formed a single file and double-timed through the airport lobby and into the Marine bus outside. It would be a 40-minute ride to Quantico. We could not hide our uneasiness. We had heard horror stories of the tough training that went on at OCS. Collectively, we focused on our goal of April 14: graduation day.

The panoramic view of the Washington Monument, Capitol Hill, and the Jefferson Memorial gave way to the forests of northern Virginia. It was a beautiful winter day. Stands of trees lifted bare branches toward a cloudless sky. Along the route we passed signs marking sites of famous Civil War battles: Manassas, Fredricksberg, Richmond.

We took the Quantico exit, off 95-South. Ahead of us, on the right side of the road, stood a small replica of the Iwo Jima memorial. Then, a large overhead sign spanned the road: THE CROSSROADS OF THE U.S. MARINE CORPS. One of the ECP candidates could not control his excitement; he stuck his head out the window and yelled, "Urah!" (the *u* pronounced like the *u* in "blue"). It was foreign to most of us at the time, but it would become familiar and necessary.

Shouted in unison, it gave us the emotional boost to climb that final hill. Said in unison, after a job well done, it reinforced a sense of solidarity.

We came to the guard station and two Marines waved us through. My heart started to beat faster. We entered the Marine Corps Development and Education Command (MCDEC), which consisted of four major training schools, including Officer Candidate School. It was the home base of the presidential helicopter squadron, and the site of the Marine Corps Air and Ground Museum. Apart from MCDEC, it also housed academies for the Drug Enforcement Agency and the FBI.

The bus drove through a forest of trees and a golf course. Three Marines in sweats were jogging on the opposite side of the street, their breath turning to steam. The bus stopped at a traffic light. A left turn would have taken us into the town of Quantico, and to the Amtrak station. I made a mental note of it, because Amtrak would be the only way back to Washington, D.C., if and when we got a 24-hour liberty.

A few minutes later, the bus turned right and rumbled across train tracks. We stopped in front of a rectangular, one-story brick building: OCS battalion headquarters. It was almost noon—1145 hours, in military parlance.

"Get the fuck out of the bus! Move, Goddamn it!"

All our heads turned in different directions searching for the source of the command. Then three sergeants dressed in heavily starched green camouflage uniforms appeared.

"Platoon formation, now!" they ordered.

The driver grinned as he swung open the door. I thought to myself, What's a platoon formation? We tumbled out of the bus in mass confusion, forming three crooked lines as the cold air hit our faces. The drill sergeants, known in Marine Corps parlance as sergeant instructors, prowled around us like mad dogs, barking unintelligible commands, trying to get us into formation. After 30 minutes there was

13

no sign of the next bus. They ordered us into the empty barracks.

"May I use the bathroom?" I nervously asked the sergeant once inside.

A look of resignation spread over his face, as he motioned with his index finger to come closer.

"In the Marine Corps it's called the 'head.' So you ask if you can make a 'head call,'" he said in a low voice.

I felt like an idiot, but to me all it meant was that I was one step closer to becoming an officer of Marines.

The rest of the candidates finally arrived. We spent the afternoon at headquarters waiting in lines and filling out forms. We each purchased a small PX (Marine Corps Exchange) bag for "health and comfort" filled with the essentials. After that there was more waiting. But the downtime provided me the opportunity to look at the 150 other candidates with whom I would be spending the next ten weeks. After being at Georgetown Law School, where 20 percent of the students were minorities, I could not help but notice the lack of them here.

We left OCS battalion headquarters and marched to our new home: OCS, Charlie Company. The defense budget cuts had drastically reduced the need for officers, so the 140th had only three platoons. As a result, Charlie Company, a three-story red brick complex overlooking the Potomac River, had room to spare. I was assigned to Second Platoon. Still dressed in our civilian clothes, we sat on our assigned beds, or racks. We were left to ourselves, but no one spoke.

"Get on line. Now!" screamed a sergeant with broad shoulders and pockmarks on his face.

There was an awkward hesitation. Most of us had no idea what he meant.

Finally, one of the ECP candidates leaped to attention on an imaginary line in front of his rack. The rest of us jumped on line and stood at attention, staring straight ahead. The sergeant screamed at us about how to act, what to wear, when to eat. In a drill to instill obedience, he made us repeatedly put on and take off our jock straps, shoes, T-shirts, trousers, skivvies. There would be, he said, a shakedown for drugs, medicines, alcohol, and weapons. I would later learn that this was "controlled stress," an important element of OCS training.

We prepared for bed. There would be no shower.

"You've got 3 minutes to make a head call and brush your teeth," the pockmarked sergeant deadpanned.

A younger blond sergeant appeared, and now both of them were in the squad bay screaming. I thought taking a crap had precedence over brushing my teeth. I made a bee-line to the rows of toilets. No partitions? What about privacy!? I stood there for a moment not knowing what to do. I heard more screaming. I whipped down my skivvies and sat . . .

"You've got 2 minutes!" yelled the blond sergeant instructor as he burst into the head. There was no way I could finish.

"Get on line now!"

"Get in your rack!" ordered the pockmarked sergeant. "What da hell's the matter with you faggots!? If you can't do this I'll send all you fags home!"

There was a chorus of creaking springs as we squirmed under our sheets and blankets. After only one day, it seemed that we were already moving with robotic precision.

"On your back . . . face the ceiling!"

More creaky springs and rustling blankets.

"Arms out of your blankets and over your chest!"

Still more sounds, followed by an eerie pause . . .

"AAAANNNNDDDD . . . SLEEP!"

The lights went off. The door to the duty hut slammed shut. The time was 2100 hours. All I could hear was the cold wind rapping against the window. I felt pressure in my bowels. I was exhausted. The memory of my life at the

Boston House, with its long, hot showers, leisurely break-fasts, and cappuccino flashed through my mind. But as I lay there I had to smile, for this is what I had wanted to do. All the screaming and stress was exactly what I had expected. I was in the Marine Corps. The 140th OCS had begun.

3

"Go Back to Your Own Country!"

Tuesday, February 7. As I stood in the mess hall line for lunch, I was still pondering about what had happened during the morning. We had been at the clinic for a medical examination. A few candidates had not passed and had been disenrolled. "They'll be flushed down to R&S platoon," a sergeant said with mocking disdain. R&S meant "Rest & Separation," a euphemism for dismissal. I shuddered to think how it would feel to be turned away at the last minute.

I had received official word that I was "good to go." After all the obstacles along the road during the application process, the relief I felt at jumping this final hurdle was indescribable. I saw four sergeant instructors milling around in the dimly lit hallway that led to the exit.

"Move, Candidate!"

"You're too damn slow!"

It was a gauntlet. Then I heard something strange.

"Nani o shiteru omae! Nani o shiteru!"

It took me a moment to realize that someone was talking to me in Japanese. I looked around and saw Master Sergeant K. M. Runyun, the senior noncommissioned officer. He was a white Marine with a tanned face prematurely lined with creases. I answered jokingly in Japanese.

It would have made sense to speak Japanese with a native speaker, or with a person with whom it is the only common language. But, as an American, to speak Japanese with a fellow American with whom I shared English as a native language, was dumb.

18 "You speak to me in Japanese, Candidate. You understand me?"

The other sergeants broke out in laughter. The sounds of the mess hall snapped me back to the present.

"Hurry!"

"Eating too slow, Candidate!"

"Goddamn it! Look straight ahead!"

I shuffled down the chow line shoulder to shoulder with other candidates, all of us anonymous and at the mercy of the sergeant instructors. I pushed my plate along the line as civilian servers filled it with spaghetti and meatballs.

"Eh, you speak English!?" came a loud voice over my shoulder.

I turned to look in the direction of the voice.

"What da hell you looking at, Candidate! You speak English!?"

"Yes, I do, Sergeant Instructor," I replied, turning only slightly in the direction of the voice.

"Well, we don't want your kind around here. . . . GO BACK TO YOUR OWN COUNTRY!" the voice bellowed in my ear.

The large mess hall grew silent. I turned to see Staff Sergeant Leland W. Hatfield, a wiry white sergeant with glasses, glaring at me. This was a first, and I was stunned. Never before had I been publicly humiliated because of my race. I didn't know how to react. I made my way to a table, sat down, and forced myself to eat. I would have given anything for a word of encouragement from a fellow candidate. Instead, I felt the prickling sensation of 150 pairs of eyes staring at me.

I had been born and raised in Hawaii, where people from so many parts of the world have come, so no one's in the majority. Growing up in the 1960s and 1970s, my friends were Japanese American like myself, but also Chinese, Korean, Filipino, Native Hawaiian, Caucasian, or a combination of any or all of the above. We shared each other's foods and cultural values; learning about those who were different was all around me. Unlike minorities on the mainland, I never felt out of place.

Hawaii's diversity comes from wave upon wave of immigrants that continues to this day. My grandparents were part of the wave of Japanese immigrants at the turn of the century. They were among thousands of people who came to fill the need for cheap labor on the sugar plantations, as new brides arranged for the plantation workers, or as skilled tradesmen, like my mother's father, who was a barber.

These first-generation immigrants, called the issei, were remarkably resilient and stoic about their difficult lives. Getting them to talk about the old days and their hardships on the plantation was next to impossible. They were at the bottom of society's heap, with the white plantation owners and managers lording it over them. Their lesson to the next generation was that success would be earned through sacrifice and hard work. They made the best of their difficult lives and complained little. They lived their values, rather than talking about them. It's a code of conduct that I've tried to live up to all my life.

Their children, my parents, part of the nisei, or second generation, saw America as a land of opportunity. Assimilating was important, but being accepted into the American mainstream wasn't their birthright. So they did their best to fit in. They studied hard, learned English, and became Christians. They didn't make waves or make trouble. My father was a perfect example. Born and raised on a sugar plantation on the Big Island, he was the first in his family to go to college on the mainland. Even though it was the Depression, with financial help from his oldest brother, Minoru, he made it to Purdue University.

This was well before the flood of international students who came to study at American universities, and my father as a Japanese American surely stuck out in West Lafayette, Indiana. But I never heard him complain about mistreatment. Instead, his memories were universally good ones. His roommate, Glenn W. Sample, became a lifelong friend; he and his wife would visit Hawaii often, bringing with them Hoosier farmers.

My father was a living example of the values of the American middle class: solid, dependable, and thrifty. After school, I would play for a while, then sit on the sidewalk to wait for him to return from his job as a bridge engineer. Every day, like clockwork, he appeared, went inside, and headed for "his" chair. He would have one, and only one, beer before dinner. His evening routine would have been equally familiar to a family in Indiana, as it was to ours in Hawaii.

Even in conformity, though, this nisei generation stood out. The heroism of the 442nd RCT, and the 100th Battalion, made up of Japanese Americans, is well documented. When the Japanese bombed Pearl Harbor, it brought the loyalty of all Japanese Americans into question. Uncle Daniel, my father's youngest brother, thirteen years his junior, was a sophomore at the University of Hawaii and a member of the Hawaii Territorial National Guard. The government ordered all Japanese Americans in the Guard to turn in their weapons. It issued Executive Order 9066, which resulted in the relocation and internment of 120,000 citizens and aliens of Japanese ancestry living on the West Coast.

On March 28, 1943, Uncle Daniel volunteered for the 442nd RCT, and was formally inducted into the United States Army. A few days later they shipped out. At the pier, Grandma Riki held her head high, stoically waving good-bye, knowing that she might never see her youngest son again. Many would never make it home. But my uncle and thousands of others like him would prove their loyalty to

Pop in the fairgrounds at Purdue University, with roommate Glenn Sample, standing on the left, 1933.

the land of their birth, fighting to make the world a better place for their children. The 442nd RCT and the 100th Battalion distinguished itself as the most highly decorated unit of its size during the war. Years later, when I entered OCS, Uncle Daniel had quietly approved of my decision.

Thursday, February 9. I was finally beginning to get my bearings. OCS Charlie Company opened out onto a courtyard and the Potomac River. The mess hall was to the left.

22

Uncle Daniel, second from left, wearing glasses and smiling into the camera, marching on Hotel Street in Honolulu with other 442nd RCT volunteers, 1943.

And to the left of the mess hall was Larson Gymnasium. There was a rust-colored footbridge that went over the railroad tracks that separated Charlie Company from the rest of the facilities. On the other side of the tracks, or "across the street," were the OCS battalion headquarters, auditorium, sick bay, parade deck, Brown PT field, obstacle course, and running trails.

The morning was spent "in-processing," which meant more lines and paperwork. The disenrollment of candidates had left some platoons larger than others, so company headquarters had ordered me to report to Third Platoon. I innocently hustled up the stairwell with my oversized green duffel bag slung over my shoulder to join my new platoon.

At the top of the stairwell stood Staff Sergeant Melvin Brice. He was built like a Coke machine: six foot, 220 pounds, square jaw, thick neck, broad shoulders. He glowered at me and chuckled. I could not have known the significance of this chance reassignment.

"Get on line."

I threw down my bag and jumped in front of the nearest rack. Brice swaggered down the squad bay with candidates at attention. He began to read from a clipboard.

"Catipon!"

"Here!"

"Cederholm!"

"Here!"

"Dupalo!"

"Here!"

He continued his swagger, barking out names. After what seemed like an eternity, he came to the end of the alphabet.

"Vargas!"

"Here!"

"Wagner!"

"Here!"

"Webster!"

"Here!"

"Woolfolk!"

"Here!"

Then Brice made a beeline for me. "What da hell is your name!"

"Candidate Yamashita, Sergeant Instructor."

"Shit," he muttered and made a quick turn.

"Hey, look, we got Yamashita!"

"What?! Yamashitee!" responded Gunnery Sergeant Charles. A. Pitts, a tall Marine with a long face.

"Damn, we got Yamashitow!" yelled out another sergeant.

It seemed everyone had their own pronunciation of my name. I stood at attention. Brice made an about face and stopped.

"Yamashita, you ever saw Ultra-man?"

The rest of the platoon broke out in laughter at this reference to a Japanese cartoon character. Remarkably, not one of the sergeants reprimanded the platoon for breaking rank. Brice continued to pace up and down the squad bay. He then stopped, and asked for a volunteer to be the platoon scribe who would post the daily list of fire team assignments. Nobody stepped forward. Brice asked for a volunteer again. No response. Finally, a young man slowly stepped forward. It was Candidate Ronnie Catipon; he was tall and handsome with a boyish face. At the time, I thought he was Latino. Later, I learned that his family had come to America from the Philippines. He accepted the added responsibility without complaint for all nine weeks of training.

Friday, February 10. In-processing continued as we were issued our camouflage uniforms, M-16 rifles, helmets, cartridge belts, and ALICE packs (All-Purpose Lightweight Individual Carrying Equipment). We purchased our large PX bag, which contained all the remaining supplies that we would need.

We were also issued Candidate Regulations that specified how the contents of our wall lockers and foot lockers would be organized. For example, camouflage uniforms, field coats, camp stools, and civilian attire needed to be stored in the wall locker. Moreover, in that wall locker, black socks, green socks, drawers, and undershirts would need to be folded to the width indicated, and placed edge forward and flush with the front of the top shelf. Personal items needed to be stored in the foot locker, and arranged neatly on the right side of the locker tray. Rifle magazines needed to be placed side by side, flaps up, in the lower right-hand corner of the tray. Brasso, marking kits, and tooth brushes to polish shoes needed to be stored on the lower left side of the tray, and arranged from left to right. Needless to say, it would be a constant challenge to keep our lockers neat and in proper order, or in Marine parlance, squared away.

The OCS chain of command was drilled into us. Third

Platoon had four sergeants: Sergeant A. K. Wade, Sergeant E. F. Carabine, Staff Seargeant Brice, and Gunnery Sergeant Pitts. They reported to the officer in charge, Lieutenant William P. Eshelman, Jr., the platoon commander. Next up the chain of command was Major Gary M. Winter, the company commander; and at the very top was the battal- ion commander, Colonel C.W. Reinke.

There would be three areas of evaluation: physical training (PT), academics, and leadership. PT would be 25 percent of the grade, academics another 25 percent, but leadership would be a whopping 50 percent of the overall evaluation. PT would be measured by a stopwatch, and academics by calculating right minus wrong. But the evaluation of leadership would be largely subjective. The most important event was the command evaluation, prepared by Lieutenant Eshelman, which accounted for 25 percent of the overall leadership grade. I would learn, nine weeks later, that this all-important evaluation would be nothing more than one man's opinion.

4

"The White Boys Still Make the Decisions"

WHEN WE WERE GROWING UP, MY PARENTS NEVER told us of their experiences with discrimination, though I knew that they had occurred. I learned about them in a roundabout way, from teachers and family friends. After my father graduated from Purdue in 1934, for instance, he returned home and applied for engineering positions in Honolulu. He soon learned that the big corporations would not hire an engineer of Japanese descent, no matter how qualified. So for three years he worked as a surveyor in a federally sponsored jobs program until he could get an engineering job with the local government. Even though he lost out on higher-paying jobs with private firms, not once did he ever voice a complaint.

When my mother returned to Hawaii after graduating from the University of Iowa, she faced a similar situation. She found that teaching positions at the University of Hawai'i were only open to whites. So she contacted her faculty adviser at the University of Iowa for help, and Professor Ruth Updigraf gave her a strong recommendation that helped nudge open the door of discrimination. She became one of three "test" minority hires in 1949, and with the exception of the time she took off after the birth of my sister, two brothers, and me, remained with the university until her retirement as an associate professor in 1994.

But these and other personal stories of discrimination were kept from us. When I would ask about the war, Mother would say, "Uncle Daniel doesn't like to talk about it." As an adult, I discovered that for decades there had been racially restricted residential areas in Honolulu. That surely meant our family had been told we couldn't live in those nice neighborhoods with big yards and beautiful homes because we were Japanese American. When I asked my mother about this, she said, "No big deal. We couldn't have afforded those homes, and I wouldn't have wanted to live there anyway."

Maybe it was denial, a defense mechanism to shield the hurt. Perhaps it was a sense of powerlessness reinforced by the Japanese phrase *shikata ga nai,* or "it can't be helped." I think, though, their reactions were based on a lifelong goal of assimilation. Discrimination, these second-generation Americans believed, would be overcome through education, hard work, and sacrifice. They thought by not dwelling on the negative, they were protecting us from the harsh realities of the world, making sure that we didn't grow up with a sense of inferiority. And in many ways they succeeded. However, as most children of nisei parents would learn, that parental silence made it difficult to recognize and to deal with discrimination. It also helps to explain my inability to identify with civil rights issues, be they Asian American, African American, gender-based, or whatever, for most of my life.

Saturday, February 11. We steeled ourselves for what lay ahead. Dressed in camouflage uniforms, we marched to OCS battalion headquarters to have our heads shaved. We entered the building, passed the PX, and lined up outside the small barber shop. There could only be three candidates in the shop at a time. Three barbers worked at breakneck speed in front of a huge mirror. On top of a small table were powders, combs, and a cardboard box where they stuffed our $3.50. Maybe it was a bargain, but the haircut was over in three minutes, and every cut was the same. I almost didn't recognize myself in the mirror. I marched out, rubbing the top of my head. Looking like Marines at last, we marched back to Charlie Company.

28   "What' ya doin' with that Irish pennant?" said Sergeant Carabine in the hallway.

I gave him a confused look. He pointed to a loose thread on my left breast pocket. He grabbed it with his fingers and with a single motion ripped it clean. I didn't stop to think that this Marine Corps' term for messy could be construed as a derogatory ethnic remark. I just kept moving.

It was time for PT. The staff ordered us to change into red nylon shorts and a yellow T-shirt emblazoned with the OCS logo. The week before we had taken an intermediate physical fitness test, which consisted of pull-ups, sit-ups, and a 3-mile run. I had passed. We marched onto Brown Field, and rested in company formation on the parade deck.

"Candidates, it's gonna be another easy day!"

There on top of a training ladder stood a British Royal Marine charged with whipping us into shape. The company gathered around him and whooped it up with shouts of "Urah" and "Marine Corps!" He was tall and lanky with a curled mustache. With his Marine green pullover sweater and English accent, he looked and sounded more like a college professor. He led us through stretching and calisthenics. At one point, he came down from his ladder, and calmly but firmly showed a couple of us what we were doing wrong. After that we completed a 3-mile run. Although I finished the run in the last third of the pack, I was relieved that there were others behind me.

Relief, though, was momentary. By the second week of OCS, Staff Sergeant Brice seemed to have made me his favorite whipping boy. He was a constant presence, ready to pounce. I could do nothing right. If he wanted to make an example of someone, it inevitably was me. I wondered if there was a connection between his hostile attitude and the earlier incidents with Sergeants Runyun and Hatfield.

Wednesday, February 15. "Yamashita, get in here . . . and pick up your eval!"

The dreaded candidate interview form, better known as the "eval," is a demerit system that is an important part of what passes for evaluation and counseling. It informs the candidate where improvement is needed, and requires him to acknowledge that he will try to correct the deficiency.

Brice was standing in front of the duty hut. I completed the form and returned it. This particular eval was for failing to secure my locker. Others would be for not being squared away, not following orders, or lacking motivation. But it seemed that these forms could have been given to anyone in the platoon. It soon became apparent that the distribution was far from consistent: while I would receive one for an infraction, another candidate would not.

Friday, February 17. Sick call. Any candidate who was sick or injured could report to company headquarters, or be referred to the battalion sick bay for more intensive care. After treatment, the candidate returned to the platoon ready to participate in all activities, or be placed on light duty or no duty status. I had pulled a groin muscle and was placed on light duty for a few days. Brice accused me of lacking motivation and gave me several eval forms. After that, I refused sick call, for it was better to deal with the pain than face Brice's rage. I found it odd that Brice said almost nothing to Kempster, a white candidate, who frequently reported to sick call and remained on light duty for weeks.

Brice's favorable treatment of Kempster struck me as particularly confusing. Growing up in Hawaii, I was taught an important value: don't make yourself look good at the expense of others. Kempster was like one of those students in school, and there's always one, who constantly raises his hand to make himself appear smarter than the rest. Unable to participate due to an injured knee, he had the audacity to bark out, not encouragement, but orders from the sidelines. Worse yet, his orders often turned out to be wrong. Yes, he was assertive. But is that leadership? In my experience, it is exactly this sort of person who will jump ship when things get rough. In my experience, it is more often than not, that quiet and unassuming individual who will fight the hardest and, when duty calls, pick up the torch himself to finish the job. A real warrior doesn't need bravado to give him an edge. I don't know whether it was personality or race, but for whatever reason, Brice liked Kempster.

Saturday, February 18. We had earned a 23-hour base liberty. This meant that we were restricted to MCDEC and the town of Quantico. If we left this area we would be considered "UA," or unauthorized absence. Brice strutted up and down the squad bay, lecturing us that we had to be clean-shaven and our civvies pressed. He went on and on for 30 minutes, cutting into our precious liberty time. I suspected he was doing it on purpose.

"Dismissed!"

I slumped down on my foot locker in front of my rack. I needed a few moments to catch my breath, physically and emotionally. Everyone else had raced down the stairwell to the basement, where we had stored our bags and civvies. Before I knew it, I was alone in the squad bay.

"Eh, Yamashita, get in here," said Brice in a low voice.

My back stiffened. I regretted not getting out of the squad bay like everyone else.

"Candidate Yamashita reporting as ordered, Sergeant Instructor!"

"Come on in," Brice said calmly. It was a tone of voice that I had never heard before.

I marched into his office, and quickly snapped to attention exactly one pace in front of his desk. The liberty that I had savored was on hold. It was the first time I had been inside the duty hut. It was a small room with four desks at each corner. Brice was sitting with his feet propped up on his desk.

"Relax, Yamashitee," he said once again in a low voice.

I noticed that the pronunciation of my name would change from moment to moment. This from the man who had been harassing me for weeks—the man who would have a large say on whether I would become an officer of Marines.

"Come on. I really mean it. Relax."

He motioned to a chair. He took his feet off the desk, leaned over, and smiled. Suddenly, he was less robotic. His thick neck and large shoulders became like those of a large teddy bear. He talked about life in the Marine Corps and the opportunities for travel and growth. He had been to Hawaii with the Corps. We talked football as he pointed to a photo of his Marine Corps team. Beaming with pride, he showed me a picture of his 5-year-old daughter. I leaned back in my chair. But then his voice took on a new urgency.

"Yamashitee—what do you see when you look at me?" he asked.

"A Marine, Sergeant Instructor."

"Don't give me that bullshit. What do you see?" I could see the old Brice returning.

My back straightened.

"A Marine, Sergeant Instructor," I insisted.

"Goddamn it, Yamashitee! You're Japanese, right?"

My shoulders tightened. "Yes, Sergeant Instructor," I said slowly.

"Now, once again. What do you see?" he asked, this time angrily pointing his index finger straight at his face.

"An African American, Sergeant Instructor?"

"Damn right! You think I make the decisions around here!?"

I sat confused, unable to respond. He leaned across the desk to answer his own question.

"No way, Yamashitee. THE WHITE BOYS STILL MAKE THE DECISIONS. AND DON'T YOU FORGET THAT!"

There must have been disbelief written all over my face. What was he telling me? Despite all of his harassment, was he now trying to tell me that we needed to stick together?

"I've been hard on you, haven't I? Well, I can make anybody look bad," he said with a hint of pride.

I nodded.

"At the end, if I like you, I repeat, IF I LIKE YOU, I'll go talk to Major Winter. And you're gonna graduate. You understand me?"

"Yes, Sergeant Instructor," I mumbled.

"Now get da hell out of here!"

I leaped to my feet, made an about face, and marched out. When I had decided to apply to OCS, Uncle Daniel had told me about his basic training in Camp Shelby, Mississippi. It was not a cheery story. He and his fellow Japanese American recruits from Hawaii and the West Coast stood out as a group, being neither white nor black. He was shocked at the racial segregation of the times: separate drinking fountains for whites and blacks, separate bathrooms. He went to movie theaters and finally understood why the balconies were called "Nigger Heaven." He had heard of an incident where a bus driver refused to pick up a black soldier who was trying to get back to base. The boys of the 442nd forced the driver to open the door and give the soldier a ride. But that had been in 1943. What was Brice talking about? This was 1989!

To complicate the meaning behind Brice's words and deeds was the changing relationship between Asian Americans and African Americans. No longer were they simply allies in civil rights struggles against white oppression. I could not assume that his conduct was benign and merely a tool to toughen me up. For as the fastest-growing minority group, Asians were increasingly seen as usurping African American political, economic, and educational

32

opportunities, and using civil rights strategies and social programs to better themselves without adequate appreciation for the sacrifices made by the African American community. In contrast, Asians saw African Americans as the beneficiaries of special privileges, and prone to scapegoating other communities instead of facing up to their own failures. On a personal level, Asians were seen as meek, cliquish, and condescending. African Americans were lazy and untrustworthy. Concrete examples of this conflict were being seen in disputes between Asian merchants and African American patrons as well as in lawsuits by Asian students demanding that admissions to public magnet high schools be based on merit and not racial quotas.

I felt that my future in the Marine Corps would depend on the answers to the questions racing through my head. Was it true that if Brice liked me I would graduate? Or was this latest encounter just another sick form of harassment? Could the Marine Corps really be a bunch of racist rednecks with Brice executing their policy? And finally, could it be possible that Brice actually resented me because I was Asian?

Quantico reminded me of the fictional town of Mayberry popularized in the 1960s sitcom, "The Andy Griffith Show." It covered about one city block, and catered mainly to the needs of Marines, OCS candidates, and other personnel on base. I caught up with Candidates Vargas, Wagner, Webster, and Woolfolk. At OCS, rack assignments are made alphabetically, so due to mere proximity, I had gotten to know them better than most of the others. They were at Quantico Pizza stuffing their faces, making up for three weeks of food deprivation. My life at the Boston House, where I would keep track of the grams of fat in my diet, seemed a lifetime away. I devoured an entire pizza and two roast beef sandwiches with fries. It was good to eat as much as I wanted, at my own pace, in peace and quiet. After a few beers, the talk turned to how I was at Brice's mercy. The beer temporarily lifted my spirits, and allowed me to see humor in the bizarre circumstances I found myself in.

"Yamashitow, quit bowing . . . this is America, man!"

"Kawasaki Yamaha Yamashita!"

The racial remarks continued, whether on the parade deck, during PT, or in the courtyard. Harassing me had become a sport, each sergeant seemingly trying to outdo the others. I could improve my academic or physical performance, but I couldn't "improve" my ancestry.

Wednesday, February 22. Academics were not going to be a problem. We had our first written examination on general military subjects. It reminded me of college entrance exams. We sat in the auditorium to take the multiple-choice test. I got a perfect score. The night compass exam was both written and applied; we spent an evening in the field locating objectives. I received a score of 90.

Although I was passing academics with ease, I particularly remember the lectures on Marine Corps history, which included wars with Japan, North Korea and North Vietnam. Normally, I would not have given it much thought, but with all the harassment surrounding my ancestry, it made me uncomfortable. It was a relief, not just for me but for everyone, when we moved on to other topics. Not that I was ashamed of my Japanese ancestry; indeed, I had come to appreciate it. But this appreciation had come slowly, and in bits and pieces. A large and significant piece came during my five years studying and working in Japan.

5

"Neither Fish Nor Fowl"

GOING FROM TOKYO TO HIROSHIMA ON THE BULLET train takes a few hours, but for me, the trip spanned generations. The year 1975 was ending, and my older sister Margaret, who was teaching English in Japan, had persuaded me to meet the relatives living there. I had taken a year off from the University of Hawaii and was spending a year abroad at the International Christian University (ICU). I had been playing hard, studying enough Japanese to get by, and resisting her pleas to see relatives I never knew, and cared little about. But winter break was coming up, and I couldn't think of a way to avoid a reunion with my distant family.

The day was bitterly cold, but waiting on the station platform was a crowd to greet us. We were in Iwakuni, a small town 70 kilometers from the city of Hiroshima. Margaret reminded me of the story behind the man we would meet: Masuto. He was the infant that my father's mother, Grandmother Riki, was forced to leave behind when she came to Hawaii with her first husband. This husband had been killed in a train accident after arriving in Hawaii. Her second marriage to my grandfather, Zenzaemon Yamashita, a laborer under contract to the plantation, had been arranged by her family back in Japan. Now in the twilight of his life, my father's half brother stepped out of the crowd. He was tall for a Japanese, and held himself with a dignity perfectly suited to his 80 years. His gentle smile reminded me of my father. And as he took my hand to shake it, he wiped away tears.

With Margaret serving as translator, I was able to communicate with him. He was a man of few words, so his wife did most of the talking. He had always felt abandoned by Grandmother Riki, even though after the war she had sent care packages year after year. When she died, he had told his family, "That's the last we'll ever hear from them." But the packages of gifts continued to arrive. And he was touched, and his heart softened. So in 1969, he had traveled to Hawaii, retracing the path his mother had taken decades earlier. Awaiting him at Honolulu Airport, leis in hand to greet him, were his half sister and three half brothers, including my father. Without hesitation, they called him *oniisan*, the honorific title for elder brother, and for the first time he felt that he was part of a family.

The day before we returned to Tokyo was an unexpectedly profound time for me. We drove along a one-lane gravel road that zigzagged up the mountainside. Two-and-a-half bumpy, heart-stopping hours later, we arrived at a remote hamlet tucked away in a tiny valley. It was the birthplace of my paternal grandfather, Zenzaemon Yamashita, and the location of the family grave. Though neither Margaret nor my mother ever said it, I realized this was the reason they had hounded me to come to Japan.

My father's cousin and his wife greeted us, and led us into a large thatch roof farmhouse surrounded by rice paddies. On Japanese-style mats they served green tea and pastries filled with black bean paste. At the family altar, there were pictures of three sons in Japanese army uniforms who had been killed in the war. After all those John Wayne movies, it was a shock to see human faces behind the enemy uniform.

After we finished our tea, they rose slowly and we followed them outside. We walked along a narrow path from the house up to the burial ground. There were numerous weather-beaten headstones. We came to the first one, and

Margaret and I with my father's half brother and his wife at Iwakuni train station, 1975.

each took turns drizzling water over it in an act of purification. This was the final resting place of my father's father's father. We lit incense and stood silently. I gazed at the stone, which bore an ancient, unreadable inscription, but felt an understanding that transcended generations. Here deep in the mountains of Yamaguchi Prefecture, I had found my roots. As I stood there, I began to appreciate the hardship endured by my grandfather who had made that long journey to Hawaii so many years before. As I stood there, my understanding of family, and my place in it, became richer and deeper. It stretched across the Pacific and reached back centuries, and would remain as strong and meaningful as I would allow it.

I had never given my racial ancestry much thought. Growing up I identified more with just being from Hawaii than anything else. From that reality, America was cool, while Japan was primitive and uncultured. But during my year abroad at ICU I had discovered a world that went far

38

beyond chopsticks and raw fish. With the eyes of an American I saw awe-inspiring art and architecture that went back hundreds of years before the pilgrims had landed at Plymouth Rock. I attended a kabuki performance, a form of theater that in its own right rivaled Shakespeare. My visit to the gravesite of my great-grandfather brought the recognition that I was not just an American outsider, but all that I had seen was part of me. Returning to Hawaii with a new-found appreciation of my own heritage, I found myself looking at friends from other backgrounds with new respect and wonder. This openness and appreciation, cultivated in Japan, had made me a better American.

But I had only scratched the surface. I needed to finish my journey of self-discovery, and complete what I had started: learn the language, be a participant, rather than just an observer of Japanese life. After graduating from the University of Hawaii, I began looking for a way to return to Japan. Luckily, I was able to secure a position in the international section of a small trading company in Tokyo. It would be a rare opportunity to live the life of a Japanese *sarariiman*, or male office worker.

When I stepped off the plane in Tokyo, I entered a world far from the typical Japanese employee. I would be staying at the president's home in Denen Chōfu, a luxurious residential area. He was called *shachō*, the honorific title for a company president. The next morning in his private car I tried to make small talk, but he appeared agitated and only grunted back. We entered a shiny building across the street from the Hotel Okura, near the American Embassy. I looked around in amazement as employees sprang to their feet to greet us with a morning chorus of "*ohayō goza-*

imasu." *Shachō* disappeared into his private office. I stood frozen and confused, uncomprehending of what I would learn was a daily ritual of subordinance.

Over the next few weeks I would make one cultural faux pas after another. Three months later, *shachō* kicked me out of his house, ordering me to report to the company dormitory located in the outskirts of Tokyo. I was not working hard enough, my Japanese was not improving fast enough, and I was making too much eye contact with him. Needless to say, I was an emotional basket case. But as misfortune often is, my eviction proved to be a blessing in disguise.

"Get up, we'll be late!"

It was Monday morning and my first Tokyo-style commute. Takashi Iwata led the way, yelling over his shoulder at me to hurry up, *"Isoge!"* It was a brisk 15-minute walk from the dorm to the neighborhood station, where we boarded a rural train to Tsudanuma. Ten minutes later we disembarked and walked to the main station to board a train for Tokyo. Masses of people descended upon the station. As soon as the train doors opened, commuters raced to get a seat.

Iwata pushed me in and whispered, "This is nothing . . . it gets worse." The train rumbled toward Tokyo. Stop after stop, hordes of people jammed their way into the car. By the time we stopped at Bakurocho there were men in uniform with white gloves ready to pack even more commuters into the train. I was standing in front of a man sitting on a seat. As I held an overhead hand strap, the crush of the crowd pushed me into his lap, my chest against his forehead.

"Adidididididididi . . ."

The sound that Japanese make when they are being jammed into the train could be heard coming from all directions. Eventually it came naturally to me too, but that day it struck me as funny. I never realized how good I had had it in the air-conditioned comfort of *shachō*'s private car. But I had come to Japan to live like the Japanese.

"Adidididididididi."

Iwata became my roommate, and with his rare sense of humor rescued me. He was from Kyoto, temporarily assigned to the Tokyo office. In his mid-50s, he spoke little English. He was wiry in build, balding, and I can still see his infectious smile. He taught me about *senpai-kōhai* and *hon'ne-tatemae*, important concepts for social interaction. He used only the simplest Japanese, patiently repeating the words for me. We would go grocery shopping together. We had drinking parties. I was his live-in valet; he became my mentor and friend.

Although life at the dormitory was good, work was hell. I was like a fish out of water, still making one cultural mistake after another. One day I felt nauseated. Then the chest pains began. Instead of asking for help, I slipped out of the office and stumbled across the street to the Hotel Okura, hoping to find an English-speaking physician. Staggering to a public phone, I tried to call for help.

After 20 frustrating minutes, I slammed the telephone receiver down. Why had I come to Japan anyway? I was a college graduate, but a Japanese 6-year-old could read and write better. I had a Japanese face, and the double take I got every time I opened my mouth was becoming a pain in the ass!

"Are you an American?"

Staring at me, looking both bemused and concerned, was a man about my father's age. He introduced himself as Peter Okada, a Japanese American businessman from Seattle. He gave me the number of his personal physician. As it turned out, I wasn't sick, just overstressed.

I didn't expect to hear from Peter again, but a week later he invited me to lunch. He knew what I was going through, and reminded me to persevere. Then he made a comment that surprised me. "You know, Bruce, you're neither fish nor fowl."

He knew I wouldn't get it, so he continued. "Here in Japan, you look the part, but you're not. In America, you

Iwata Buchō at the dormitory, 1981.

act the part, but you're not. I know," he said ruefully, "because it's the same with me."

That forced me to think about what I was experiencing, and the problems trying to turn myself into a loyal Japanese employee. It wasn't that I refused to accept the rules of conduct for the typical *salariiman*, but a life's worth of hearing about the value of the individual and the Western concept of respect was a lot to overcome in a few short months. I was learning much about Japanese culture, but I was finding that there were things I could neither accept nor understand.

Two weeks later, I was fired. The humiliation gave way to relief. Now riding the train in the opposite direction of the rush-hour commute, I thought, This is what I need to do with my life. I would buck the tide of social conformity and follow my heart. I found a tiny apartment in Tokyo, and used a kerosene stove for heat. I bought a bicycle, which became my mode of transportation. I was living in poverty, but I was free!

Over the next few weeks, I ended my social isolation. I contacted George Sakamoto, a friend from ICU, who had gone to high school in Hawaii, and was now working at Mitsubishi Trading Company. We met another friend from ICU, who brought along his two younger sisters. With George as the organizer, this core group of friends flourished. It would include company workers, students, photographers, journalists, artists, government workers, academicians, and foreign expatriates. It was a loose, informal group engaged mostly in drinking and carousing, but it also provided business contacts, opportunities for romance, and, in one case, a proposal for marriage.

Because we were young and in a foreign land, there were times when the carousing went too far. Sasaki was a freelance photographer, and he behaved like the stereotypical artist. His finances were those of an artist as well, which meant neither of us had much money; having a good time required ingenuity. Looking back, I shudder at our shared audacity. We would go to a cheap *yakitoriya*, a Japanese-style bar and grill, and sit next to a group of rowdy *salariman*. They would always leave unfinished bottles of beer and plates of food. Sasaki taught me to discreetly confiscate the leftovers from adjoining tables before waiters could clear them. If we were careful, we could eat and drink until dawn without breaking our meager budgets.

Never a paragon of restraint, Sasaki could spiral out of control. One night, we went through our usual routine, and I decided it was time to go home. He would not hear of it, protesting the way he did almost every time we got together. But this time I ignored him. He stumbled after me.

"Eh, you, let's drink!"

He followed me to my apartment, threatening bodily harm if I didn't return. I slammed the door. He pounded on it. I swung the door open, shoving him down the stairs. He knocked over a garbage can, sending it crashing across the quiet street. He picked up the metal cover and came after

George Sakamoto, standing in the back, and myself to his left, with the core group of friends in Tokyo, 1982.

me. I ducked, closed my eyes, and swung. A voice yelled out that the cops were on their way. Sasaki disappeared into the night, tears streaming down his bloodied cheek.

Although my Japanese had improved, I was still in a linguistic fog. I was frustrated that I was unable to find suitable reading material: children's books were boring; adult newspapers were too difficult to read. I suspected there must be other foreigners in the same boat. I met with Ikuo Nakanishi, the principal of the Aoyama School of Japanese where I had been a part-time student. We talked about a newspaper aimed at the adult learner, but written in a simpler style and with less *kanji*, or Chinese characters. If I would be the editor, he promised to give me a tuition waiver, a stipend, and total control over content and format. His only request was that the staff be comprised of not just Americans and Europeans. He wanted diversity.

The *Yokomeshi Shinbum* was born with little but hope. I assembled a diverse staff where, more often than not, the only common language was Japanese. But I conveyed to them the value of finding common ground and the importance of overcoming our differences.

I had learned this growing up in Hawaii—not just because of its diversity, but because I found myself in situations where I had to get along and respect others. Since I was 6 years old I played little league baseball. At 10 I began playing Pop Warner Football. Most of the kids on those teams went to large public schools. Many came from different backgrounds ethnically, socially, economically. I still remember my Samoan Pop Warner football coach inviting us to his home for lunch in one of the poorest neighborhoods of Honolulu. I recall visiting a baseball teammate's home which was not much more than a shack. For many of them going on to college and graduate school were not in their futures. But we learned from each other. We shared with each other. We became friends. We became a team, and we won a few championships along the way.

I was beginning to find my niche. An article published in the *Yokomeshi* on the Sanya district in Tokyo; the sordid underbelly of the city where the homeless gathered, attracted considerable media coverage: radio, TV, magazines. After a radio interview, the disc jockey invited me for drinks. We went from one bar to another. As I stumbled into the taxi, he told me that I would be perfect for a radio show that his station was producing. He made good on his promise, and put me on the air to help with a program that introduced American "Top 40" music. The parties and public appearances led to more DJ jobs and live events. The mundane life of a Japanese *salariman* was forgotten in a new rush of show business glitter.

By this time I had a steady girlfriend, Mari Saito, a graduate of ICU. She was bilingual and bicultural, having gone to high school in New York. My fondest memory was a trip we took to Hakone, a popular vacation resort. We stayed at a traditional Japanese inn. We put on the light cotton *yukata* and warm *tanzen* that we had found waiting for us in our room. The maid brought us our dinner on individual trays: a feast for the eyes as well as the palate. We had a private garden overlooking a stream with a forest of pine trees. In the middle of the garden was our own private *rotemburo*, an outdoor hot spring. After dinner we sat in the warm bath. The cold air turned our breath to steam. We drank hot *sake*, gazed at the stream below, and listened to the silence of the forest. As we sat there we laughed and enjoyed the moment. We were young without a care in the world. Filled with potential and possibility, it was great to be alive!

45

I had finally succeeded in navigating through Japanese society. I would go for months without speaking English. My domestic and foreign news came from the Japanese press. For the first time I saw the world from another cultural and linguistic perspective. And the hard work we put into the *Yokomeshi* paid off. It was being sold at major bookstores in Tokyo. It had subscribers from Asia, Europe, and America. It was being used by teachers of Japanese, both in Japan and abroad.

It had been an incredible four years, but I could hear America calling me home. Although I could move in and out of different social groups, the truth was that I still felt detached. No matter how good my Japanese had become, there were times when I couldn't understand; no matter how comfortable I became with the cultural norms and behaviors, I would still unknowingly violate one social rule or another. Ironically, by deepening my understanding of the Japanese language and culture, I had come to appreciate how American I really was.

Before I left Japan, I made a return trip to see my relatives in Iwakuni. Now I could speak with them without an interpreter. With gentle prodding, they shared with me their firsthand account of the atomic blast over Hiroshima. I, in turn, shared my parents' memories of the attack on Pearl Harbor. My first trip helped me discover my roots; this trip reminded me how far I had come. On the day of my return, everyone was on the train platform to see me off. But now they were not nameless faces. They were an aunt and an uncle, cousins, and their children. Although our experiences were worlds apart, we shared a familial tie that transcended time and place. There were a lot of tears that day. But for me they were not tears that came from sadness, but from knowing that this marked the pinnacle of an exhilarating journey of self-discovery.

46

6

"Urah!"

"No . . . no . . . you get into the big man's line" said Carabine, a muscular white sergeant no taller than I, who raced toward me and glared in my face.

Friday, February 24. It was our turn on the obstacle course, 100 yards of agony that had brought down many a candidate, by either failure or injury. The Royal Marine had led us through our usual warm-ups. As we had marched toward the course, it seemed to loom larger and larger. The initial event required a candidate to maneuver over a preliminary obstacle, jump up and grab a bar high overhead, and swing onto the course. They had separated us into three lines depending on height. I had been assigned to the line all the way to the right, where the lowest bar hung. My heart was pounding. That's when Carabine had ordered me into the big man's line. I hesitated.

"Goddamn it, Yamashitow . . . get into the other line!"

The rest of the candidates looked on without saying a word. I slowly moved to the line where candidates towered over me. I inched toward the front. I completed the preliminary obstacle and then looked up at the bar. It looked so far away . . .

"Jump! Jump! Goddamn it. Jump!"

I hesitated.

"Jump! Goddamn it!" he yelled, his face turning red.

It was cold. I was tired. He was screaming in my ear. I jumped. A pain shot through my shoulder as I crumpled to the sawdust pit below. As the corps man helped me onto a jeep, I saw Carabine glaring at me from across the field. My dream of being a Marine was over. I would be disenrolled due to injury, and sent to the dreaded R&S platoon. But at sick bay the attending physician concluded that it was nothing serious. He gave me motrin, which reduced the pain but did nothing for the humiliation. I went to sleep that night reliving it over and over. If I could have just reached the bar . . .

The pace at OCS accelerated. The next several days they pushed us to our limits. We were hungry. We were sleepy. Our bodies ached. Already a number of candidates had quit. There were rumors that Candidate McClendon, a black candidate and ECP, had requested mast. Through whispers in the squad bay, I concluded that it was a formal procedure that allows a candidate to go over his superior and meet someone higher in the chain of command. Although the sergeants had not subjected him to racial remarks, they had picked on him from the start. He, too, had received numerous eval forms. It all happened very quickly. I returned to the squad bay and saw his foot locker empty and mattress rolled up on his rack. There were rumors as to what had happened, but no one really knew. Whatever the case, the message was clear: if I wanted to graduate, I had better keep my head low and my mouth shut.

Monday, February 27. Brice instructed the platoon on drill: how to march in step, keep straight lines, and perform the manual of arms. Brice swaggered from one side to the other, lecturing us on the proper way to handle an M-16. He wielded the 8-pound weapon as if it were a match stick.

"Ten hut!" he suddenly yelled.

He stopped, looked over the platoon, and walked toward me.

Uncle Daniel, second row, standing in the center, at Camp Shelby, member of Third Battalion, "I" Company, before the 442nd RCT was ordered into combat, 1943.

"Eh, Yamashitee . . . you know during World War II . . . were the Russians and the Japanese ever at war?"

My back stiffened. I frantically reviewed my world history.

"Yes, Sergeant Instructor," I finally blurted.

I could see him out of the corner of my left eye. He came up to my face.

"No way, Yamashitee. . . . WE WHIPPED YOUR JAPANESE ASS!"

I wonder if Staff Sergeant Brice fully appreciated the painful irony his words evoked. In April 1944, America was at war with Japan, but at the same time, the European campaign was reaching a crucial juncture. After a year of training, the 442nd Regimental Combat Team finally received its orders into combat. It was two months before the invasion of Normandy. Uncle Daniel along with the rest of the newly trained recruits boarded ships. England? Africa? The Pacific? Rumors were rampant.

Their ship passed through the Mediterranean Sea, and headed for Naples, Italy, where they hooked up with the 100th Battalion, which had been fighting along the Italian coast for months. Early July 1944, the 442nd RCT had fought their way north. The Germans had pushed them out of a valley, and pinned them down in a wheatfield. But the combat-hardened 100th Battalion had launched a counter-attack. They had cut off the enemy and had bombarded their positions with heavy artillery. The fighting had been fierce. Uncle Daniel recalls seeing the bodies of fellow American soldiers as well as those of the enemy as he trudged out of the valley. Buddies had died, but by the grace of God, many had survived.

Thursday, March 2. We marched to the large auditorium. It would be a break from the normal routine. We were there to get our uniforms for the graduation ceremony. This would require several fittings, with the final one during the last week of OCS. But these uniforms were not issued to us; we had to purchase them ourselves. So Marine Corps protocol was left at the door, and the marketplace took over. Suddenly, I felt like I was at a shopping mall. Each vendor used the same marketing technique: a young woman assistant. I made a beeline to a petite brunette who spoke with a Southern drawl. After four weeks of OCS, just seeing a woman was a treat. When she learned I was from Hawaii, her business manner became friendly. We chatted a bit as she measured my neck and shoulders, and helped me put on the olive green Service "A" coat. The abstract goal of becoming an officer of Marines had suddenly become real.

That evening it was back to the usual grind. Gunnery Sergeant Pitts, a black Marine, led us through the normal routine. This was unusual, for he normally stayed in the background. Pitts was technically the platoon sergeant, but Brice ran the day-to-day activities. The rumor was that Pitts had only recently been assigned to OCS, and was still learning the ropes.

It was clear that Brice was the more talented of the two. He had star power. He could enter a room and change its dynamics. He was massive with an intense physical presence. Far more than Pitts, he was the sergeant that the other cadre looked to for guidance.

We had 10 minutes to shower. Five minutes to change into our skivvies and T-shirts. Then we stood on line at attention with elbows against our sides, forearms and hands outstretched. Pitts walked down the squad bay inspecting each candidate, which included a search for dirt under the fingernails. Candidate Catipon, as the platoon scribe, completed the list of fire team duty assignments for the night. Pitts gave us only a moment to review the list.

"In the racks!"

I jumped in and crawled under the blanket.

"ANNNNND SLEEEP!"

The door to the duty hut slammed shut. "Lights out" was at 2100 hours, but most of us didn't get to sleep until well after midnight. Instead, we studied, spit-shined our boots, or took a shit—all the things that we didn't have time to do during the day.

I felt a tug on my leg. It was Candidate Wright, my rackmate. We had fire team duty from 0300–0400 hours. Our responsibility was to patrol the squad bay, making sure that the lockers were secure, helmets were hanging on the side of the racks, and all was in order. I dragged my body out of bed, momentarily fumbling in the dark before changing into my cammies, cartridge belt, and two full canteens. The sound of snoring filled the room.

The squad bay was rectangular, about 80 feet long with twelve racks lined up on each side of the room. In front of each rack was a foot locker, and behind it a wall locker. In the corner of the squad bay was a bulletin board where they allowed us to put up pictures of wives and girlfriends. I didn't have either, so I taped a photo of Margaret's two sons, Billy, 4 years old, and Teddy, 2. When things got rough, I would gaze at their pictures and think of home.

Although fire team duty robbed me of sleep, it did give me a rare moment of solitude. As I approached the end of the squad bay, I paused to look out the window. A single floodlight illuminated the courtyard below. The wind made the snow dance in feathery swirls. The bare branches of the maple tree outside the window framed the Potomac River, which flowed dark and eerie in the distance. As I stood there I reflected on the routine we had settled into: reveille at 0500 and then on the go all day long. We averaged 4 hours of sleep. We only had 15 minutes to eat. Everything was a blur: the yelling, the PTs, the classes. I took solace in the fact that graduation day, April 14, was in sight. I continued patrolling the squad bay, but before I knew it an hour had past. It was almost 0400. Time to wake up the next team: Candidates Catipon and Cederholm.

I was taking off my boots when Cederholm tapped me on the shoulder. He was the All-American kid, the sort of person that parents would want their children to become friends with. He had come to OCS right after college. His father was an officer in the Marine Corps Reserves. He was tall and handsome, with light brown hair.

"I gotta tell you. Whenever I get down, I think of all the bullshit you're taking, and it motivates me," he whispered. "Urah!"

"Urah!" I replied in a hushed voice.

I smiled, buoyed by the fact that my efforts were being recognized. I was convinced that the racial harassment was simply a good-intentioned test of my mettle.

52

7

"Leadership in Action"

My sister Margaret, brothers Allen and David, and I enjoyed a classic American childhood. We were sansei, the third generation in America. We watched the same television shows as mainland kids, although we saw them weeks later because the tapes had to be sent to Hawaii for broadcast. My mother took us to a parade to see President John F. Kennedy when he visited Hawaii. We learned the same lessons about the value of hard work and the importance of education. We heard the same clichés about America being the land of equal opportunity regardless of race, creed, or color. And we believed them.

Because we believed them, when confronted with the racism of the real world, we often didn't know how to react. It's common among people from Hawaii who leave for vacations, school, or jobs. We're not accustomed to the subtle signs of discrimination: when a hotel clerk tells us he can't honor our reservation, then suddenly finds a vacancy for the businessman who walks in after us; when an apartment advertised for rent isn't available, but is rented to another couple; when we're pointedly ignored in a restaurant while others around us are being served. We're not used to such treatment based on race. When it finally sinks in, we're shocked. And if we're the victim of an overtly racist act, it's incomprehensible.

The Yamashita family growing up in Hawaii. I am the one being carried, 1957.

As a child, I never understood what my fourth grade teacher was trying to say about racism. Mr. Lee was a retired Air Force pilot, stern and with an authoritative bearing. An Asian, he was teaching a class of mostly Asian children at the height of the civil rights struggle on the mainland. I knew a few white kids, but I didn't know any blacks. Neither did my classmates. So we weren't interested, and we couldn't relate.

It was important to Mr. Lee, though. He wanted us to feel the urgency he felt. Maybe he was recalling a particular insult he had suffered, or maybe he was just frustrated with us, but in the middle of explaining Dr. Martin Luther King's March on Washington, he stopped, wheeled about, snapped his arm out, and pointed, rapid-fire. At me. At the others.

"How does a white man address a black man?" he bellowed.

Two dozen 10-year-olds carefully avoided their teacher's eyes, then snuck discreet glances at one another. We were afraid to speak. We squirmed in our chairs. I thought something in Mr. Lee had snapped.

"How does a white man address a black man?" he repeated, then screamed,

"Eh, BOY! Get over here, BOY!"

The lesson was over. None of us had a clue as to what it meant. We'd never seen this on the "Adventures of Ozzie and Harriet." From the back of the room came a giggle. But the rest of us sat in silence, bewildered as to what had taken place. Mr. Lee glowered at us for what seemed like an eternity. Both he, and we, were saved by the bell.

Wednesday, March 8. The past several days had been a whirlwind of PT, academic classes, and graded events. I was ordered to appear at the fifth week review board. The day before I had passed SULE I (Small Unit Leadership Exam), but my peer evaluation had sealed my fate. I tried to ignore it, but the staff's racial remarks and unfair treatment had sent the message that they didn't want me around. No wonder I had gotten a little nervous when Brice passed out blank chits to our squad, and ordered us to rate each other based on "who we would want to go into combat with?" My squad rated me 14 out of 14 . . . dead last.

For weeks we had been anxious about who would be ordered to appear before the review board. It was the official vehicle to notify a candidate of substandard performance. There would also be boards during the seventh and ninth weeks, and a final one before the battalion commander, Colonel Reinke. This initial review board was held in the office of Major Winter, the company commander. I and ten other candidates from Third Platoon nervously stood in line, looking straight ahead.

Right in front of me was Vargas. He was born in Bolivia, of medium height and stocky. He had a black belt in the martial arts, and knew more than I about drill, weapons, and formations. I would rely on him for information and advice. Although our predicament created a bond between us, I also felt a competition. I couldn't help but think that the more the staff went after him, the less time they would have for me.

"Yamashita!"

I made my way to the door of Major Winter's office.

"Candidate Yamashita, reporting as ordered, Sir!"

Major Winter was a large man with broad shoulders. From behind his desk he looked right through me. Seated next to him was Captain R. P. Mortenson, company executive officer; Lieutenant Eshleman, my platoon commander; and Master Sergeant Runyun, company first sergeant. I noticed that although the enlisted ranks had numerous minorities, the officer corps was white. The review was brief.

"Are you being treated fairly!?"

"Do you wanna quit!?"

Major Winter placed me on company probation. I ran up the stairwell determined to improve. What I didn't know was that the worst was yet to come.

Sunday, March 12. Greg Slone, a friend from law school, was driving me back to OCS. We spoke little. My thoughts were focused on what had happened the day before. The company had been given a 23-hour normal liberty, which meant that, unlike base liberty, we could escape up to 80 miles away from OCS. I had made arrangements for Greg to pick me up in Quantico so that we could drive up to Washington for dinner. While I had been waiting for him, I used a public phone to call Mother and Pop. She was still teaching at the University of Hawaii. Pop had finally retired from the State of Hawaii as head bridge engineer. I admitted that things were rough, but didn't mention the derogatory racial remarks. I didn't want them to worry. Instead, I assured them that I was okay, and would see them soon.

As I had stood on the street corner waiting for my ride, three enlisted Marines walked into Quantico Pizza. They had pointed at me and laughed.

"Eh, look, it's Yamashitee!"

Apparently, the sergeant instructors had repeated "Yamashitee" stories so that my name and face had become known beyond the 140th OCS. I had turned away, wondering how this notoriety would affect my future as a Marine. Was it really just a test, harmless in the end? I convinced myself that I was being hypersensitive. I'd take it in stride, and worry about more important things, like my performance.

Greg dropped me off. I ran up to the squad bay. A few candidates had returned early to store and clean their personal gear. As I walked toward my rack, I noticed several of them hovering around an article. "So what's up?" I asked as I passed.

All eyes were on me. They were reading an article on war crimes perpetrated by General Tomoyuki Yamashita of the Imperial Japanese Army during World War II. Another time and place, I would have read the article myself with interest. I probably would have mentioned lightheartedly that in Japan the last name Yamashita is as common as Johnson or Smith in the United States. But with all that had been going on at OCS, I was in no mood for jokes.

"Are you related to this guy?" one candidate finally asked.

"Nope," I said without expression, and walked on.

Monday, March 13. Already the rumor had spread throughout the platoon. Over the weekend, one of the candidates had returned to the squad bay late in the evening. In the stairwell, he had noticed the odor of alcohol and perfume. At the entrance to the squad bay, he ran into a startled Staff Sergeant Brice. He was drunk. But even more shocking was that he was not alone. There was a young woman with him. According to an ECP, women and booze in the duty hut were against regulations. Of course, it was just a rumor. Nothing was ever substantiated. But it was another sign, whether I wanted to see it or not, that things were spiraling out of control, and that perhaps the regulations—including the ones to protect me—were meaningless.

Saturday, March 18. Lieutenant Eshelman called me into his office. That week I had failed the practice endurance run. It required the candidate to complete in 43 minutes the obstacle course, 3-mile run, stamina course, and partial combat course. Candidates Catipon, Webster, and a few others had also failed. It is a grueling event, the culmination of our physical training. A passing score is 43 minutes. I ran a disappointing 43:26.

"You gotta pass the endurance run, it's a major physical event."

"Aye, aye, Sir."

"And the obstacle course, you gotta pass that too."

Lieutenant Eshelman was slight of build, almost intellectual in appearance. But he was in top physical shape, with a neatly cropped "high and tight," a crew cut with the sides and back of the head shaved smooth, leaving only a half an inch or less of hair on the top. On one level we were very different. He was young, 25 or 26 years old at the most. Rumor had it that he was a Marine general's son; enlisting in the Marine Corps was expected of him. He would carry on the family tradition. I could not help but think that while for me the path to entering the Marine

Corps would be strewn with obstacles, for him the gates were wide open. But on another level we had a lot in common. I had heard that he was a graduate of Purdue University. Had I met him under different circumstances, we probably would have ended up swapping Hoosier stories. Moreover, I felt an affinity with him that I didn't have with the enlisted corps. He was a college graduate, and in terms of outward appearances and demeanor, would have blended into any of my law school classes.

59

"Are you being treated fairly by the sergeants?" he continued.

"Yes, Sir."

The question was just for show. He had left the door wide open. Brice, Pitts, Wade, and Carabine were at their desks outside and could hear everything that was being said. By this time, every candidate knew that complaining about the sergeant instructors would not be tolerated. We all remembered the lesson of Candidate McClendon.

As I stood there, I began to suspect that the OCS command had condoned the racial remarks and unfair treatment. I often saw Lieutenant Eshelman in the mess hall, in the auditorium, during marches, or on the PT field. It would be hard for him to claim that he wasn't aware that his staff was using racial epithets and unfairly singling out specific candidates. By allowing it to continue, he became a party to it.

Years later I would meet a Latino officer who had slurs hurled at him on the first day of Army OCS. He could never forget how the young platoon commander had reprimanded the offending sergeant, which put an immediate end to such conduct. Later he had the privilege of becoming a trainer at an Army school. The commanding officer had lectured them at a briefing about professionalism and the abuse of power. He spoke about the integrity of the system, and the importance of allowing every soldier a fair opportunity to succeed. Leadership that was simple and powerful. The sort of leadership that did not seem to exist at the 140th OCS.

"Dismissed," Eshelman said without emotion.

I made an about face and marched out of the office.

I saw Sergeant G. Carrasco coming toward me down the hall. He was short and stocky with glasses. Whenever he addressed me, he would link my name with that of a Japanese product. I avoided eye contact, hoping to pass without incident.

"Hey, Kawasaki Yamashita . . . you really Japanese?"

My face tightened as I came to attention. "Yes, Sergeant Instructor . . . Japanese AMERICAN."

"Oh, kinda like me, huh . . . I'm Mexican American." He gave an encouraging smile. I suspected that Carrasco bore me no animosity. He was at the bottom of the chain of command. By now, things had turned into a feeding frenzy, with me as the entrée. The OCS leadership had whipped the troops into line, and everyone down to Carrasco had fallen in. It was taking its toll on me, and it came straight from the top. It was, I thought, Marine Corps leadership in action—but it was the sort of leadership I didn't understand.

8

"The Workhorse"

"KAWASAKI, YAMAHA, YAMASHITA."

"Quit bowing, this is America, man!"

"Sorry, Yamashita, but we have no tea or sushi here."

The racial remarks continued, even increased. On Sunday, March 19, I was in the mop basin cleaning my weapon by running hot water over the barrel and chamber. I was sharing the faucet with Candidate O'Brien, an ECP from rural Nebraska.

"Can I ask you a personal question, Yamashita?" he asked hesitantly.

I nodded.

"Why didn't you just join the Japanese Army?"

At first I was convinced that I had misunderstood the question. After a moment, I explained that I had been born and raised in America, and that I was an American. O'Brien gave me a confused look and walked away. In a way, I couldn't blame the O'Briens of the platoon for thinking of me as a foreigner, after all that Brice and the others had said. But I also knew that six weeks into OCS, for a candidate to ask such an odd question was not a good sign. And I felt a pang of fear that after being singled out week after week, there would eventually be a price to pay.

Later that day, we were on the combat course, where instructors evaluated our tactical skills while on a battlefield.

It was cold, and we had been warned of the dangers of hypothermia. The staff chose me as one of several fire team leaders. We were instructed to lead our teams to an enemy position on a hill. We would be using blanks, not live ammunition. OCS staff were stationed at various points along the course. Seargeant Wade, a short, but muscular black Marine, attached himself to my team, harassing us every step of the way. In the weeks before, Wade had taken infantile pleasure in sneaking up behind me and yelling, "Boo! Hey! or Yamashitee!" My startled reaction would always get a thunderous laugh from him. I wondered whether he had forgotten that this was supposed to be Marine Corps training, not summer camp.

We approached the obstacles. I implored my team to keep moving. I entered the quigley, a water obstacle, with my weapon above my head. A candidate ahead of me had collapsed, apparently from hypothermia. My body began to quiver and then became numb. I exited the other side gasping for air. I crawled out of the water with my body shaking uncontrollably.

"No, Yamashitee, do it again!" Wade yelled, looking down at me.

As I maneuvered through the quigley again, Wade laughed with delight.

The obstacles continued up a hill. Overs and unders. Back crawl. Cliff climb. High and low walls. The ford. When I approached the hill, I gave the signal to disperse and fire at a machine gun nest in a fire hole. But as I came closer to the objective, I ran out of ammunition. For any other candidate this would have gone unnoticed. But Wade was watching my every move.

"So what you gonna do, Yamashitee, what you gonna do?!" he yelled, rushing up to me and sticking his nose in my face.

I was confused. Whether I had ammo was not important.

Heck, I could have just said, "Bang!" What was important was that I had led my team to the objective.

"Goddamn it, do something!" he screamed.

I charged, and jumped into the fire hole ready for hand-to-hand combat. I did what I thought any good Marine would have done. But Seargeant Wade went berserk. As I stood at attention, shivering in the cold, he berated me in front of everyone. For the next week Wade and Carabine took great delight in calling me the "Kamikaze Man." I was beginning to feel that I was in a no-win situation. No matter what I did, it would be wrong.

Later in the solitude of my rack an inner voice told me to give the OCS staff the benefit of the doubt. I spurred myself on with the belief that they had my best interest at heart. Quitting never entered my mind. I would make it through OCS, as long as I continued to improve.

My childhood was filled with lessons on the virtue of perseverance. Since my mother was a professor at the University of Hawaii, all of us children were able to attend the University's Laboratory School on campus. The Lab School was exactly that: a combination training ground and research facility for the College of Education. All through school I knew this was a different place, but didn't fully appreciate it until well after I was gone.

Small and progressive, the Lab School was a nurturing place. I knew everybody, and everybody knew me. Teachers were always encouraging us to do better. In second grade, I was in the lowest reading group, and for Mrs. Vivian Chang, that was unacceptable. Her hair was straight and bluntly cut; she spoke quickly and abruptly. But she was dedicated and compassionate. She recommended I get glasses to read better. She made me redo assignments again and again. I still didn't make the honor roll, but she pushed me to do my best.

Despite the efforts of Mrs. Chang and my other teachers, I was never the best of students, probably for lack of interest. Sports, though, was another matter. I wanted to play football, but the Lab School was too small to field a team. Then the head coach at Iolani, a private preparatory school, after seeing me play in a Pop Warner game, approached me to play for him. I agreed to transfer, but as luck would have it, the Lab School and three other schools had banded together to create a joint football team called the HUMMERS, a combination of Hawaii Baptist Academy, University Lab School, Maryknoll School, and Mid-Pacific Institute. I had already committed to Iolani and my father had paid a nonrefundable semester's tuition. Mother, though, admonished that "life is too short to have regrets," and convinced him to allow me to return to the Lab School.

Little did I know what I was getting myself into. We would be playing established private high schools with traditions of winning football. Our head coach was Leon Schumacher, a former linebacker for the Pittsburgh Steelers. The team's only asset was his optimism. He had no coaching staff. He had no weight room. Even the name of the team didn't exactly sound ferocious.

That first season was long and comical. Some teammates didn't even know how to put on their shoulder pads. At our practice scrimmages there weren't enough helmets to go around, so when the offensive team ran off the field, they would have to pass their helmets to incoming defensive players. Our fully equipped opponents would watch in disbelief. During the season the opposing team's pep squad would mockingly sing "HUMMMMMMMMMMMM" as we took the field. At one game, in another lopsided slaughter, the public address announcer added insult to injury by referring to us as the "Humdingers." But we worked hard, and slowly began to resemble a team. The highlight of our season was our final game against Iolani. They thought I was a traitor for leaving them, and I admit they had a point. What began as a grudge match turned into an upset. I scored a touchdown, and we had our first win ever.

64

This is me running for glory. As you can tell by the reaction of the bench, scoring a touchdown and winning did not come often for the HUMMERS, 1970.

My senior year we finally fielded a varsity team. It was less a game of football than a remarkable lesson in perseverance. I was the team co-captain, and we were blown out every game. After every lopsided loss, Coach Schumacher gave us different versions of his pep talk. He reminded us that we couldn't be winners all the time. He talked about not giving up. He talked about character. He reminded us that it's easy to be a winner on Saturday, and then practice on Monday, but hard when you lose week in and week out. The over-riding message was clear: we started the season, and, come hell or high water, we were going to finish it. I'd listen, but thought we deserved at least one victory to ease the pain, both physical and emotional.

In a way, perseverance did pay off. At the end of the season, I was the third leading rusher in the league, and was selected to be on the *Honolulu Star-Bulletin* and *Honolulu Advertiser* Second All-Star Team. Looking back I probably didn't receive this recognition because of my on-the-field achievement. It must have been my tenacity. I had more carries than anyone else that year. One sportswriter nicknamed me "The Workhorse," and it stuck. I would learn that Coach Schumacher, who had made me lift weights and run extra laps since the day I met him, lobbied for my selection. More evidence, I believed, that authority figures who pushed me to my limit really had my best interest at heart.

66

The next year the team added a fifth school, got a new coach, and changed its name to Pac-Five. Several years later they accomplished the unthinkable: they won the state championship. I had to smile, for I couldn't help but think that a piece of that championship somehow belonged to Coach Schumacher, and his pioneer, never-say-die, ragtag band of Hummers.

9

"Do You Wanna Quit?"

MONDAY, MARCH 20. THE BIVOUAC. WE HAD PRE-
pared for this with a series of conditioning hikes that
required candidates to demonstrate march procedures
under physical and mental stress. But a virus was going
around the squad bay that left many of us coughing and
sneezing. Some of the candidates complained of a fever. We
trudged to the landing strip adjacent to Larson Gymnasium. We were dressed in our cammies, field coats, helmets,
and boots. We wore on our backs ALICE packs, which had
collapsable shovels and camp stools secured to the outside.
We also had cartridge belts with two full canteens, and
M-16s slung over our right shoulders.

The whirring sound grew louder as the helicopter
approached. Soon, the noise became deafening. The chopper landed and the back flung open. With the sergeants
screaming all around us, we ran under the rotating blades,
and the entire platoon jammed into its cavernous belly. It
slowly lifted off the ground and headed out over Brown
Field toward the mountains beyond. The word was that we
would hump it back. By the time I was able to peer out the
window, OCS was in the distance. I anxiously looked at the
miles and miles of forest below. I knew the longer we flew,
the longer the hump back would be. Finally, mercifully, the

chopper circled and landed in an open area sandwiched between two hills. The back opened, and we scrambled out.

It wasn't the best day for a bivouac. The field was muddy. There were dark clouds overhead. Our first task was to make rows of two-person tents. I was teamed with Candidate Marcayda. I took out the shelter half, pins, guide lines, and poles from my ALICE pack. Marcayda and I joined our shelter halves to form a small tent, securing it to the ground with pins. By the time we were finished, our cammies were wet, our boots and socks caked with mud.

Evening brought freezing cold. The good news was that we would not have to eat an MRE (Meals Ready to Eat)— dry food in foil bags that tasted like cardboard with vitamins. The mess staff had been flown in to prepare a hot meal. We sat outside on our lightweight aluminum-framed camp stools and ate. The temperature continued to drop. The platoon spread out into the surrounding area to gather wood for the bonfire. Candidate Wagner and I walked deep into the forest. He was from Indianapolis, so we talked about Indiana basketball. He was married and on an aviation contract. He was quiet, and appeared more serious about his future goals than some of the others. But he was always ready to lend a hand or give a word of encouragement. About 20 minutes later we proudly lugged back a large tree stump. For a moment the rigors of OCS were forgotten, and memories of YMCA overnight camps were revived. Even the sergeant instructors seemed more relaxed.

At 2100 hours, it was lights out. I snuggled into my sleeping bag trying to stay warm even though my uniform was still damp. By this time the temperature was just above freezing. Then it started to rain and water was seeping under the edges of our tent. I then felt an uncomfortable pressure in my bowels. I had missed latrine call. There would be no time the next day, and I had to go. I could have flagged down the fire team to request an escort to the bushes. But if I did that, Brice might find out, and only God knows what his reaction would be.

There was no moon out. I fumbled through my ALICE pack for my flashlight. My hands were growing numb with cold. Candidate Marcayda was snoring. I quietly pulled myself out of my sleeping bag, and grabbed my E-tool. I dug a shallow hole in the pouring rain right outside our tent, expecting Brice to appear at any moment. With water dripping down my forehead, and feeling like a dog in the rain, I did my thing. There was no toilet paper. I quickly filled in the hole, and returned to my sleeping bag, drenched and shivering. I still had a cold and was hacking up phlegm. As I slid into my sleeping bag, I focused on the fact that on April 14 the nightmare would be over. On April 14, I would be an officer of Marines.

Tuesday, March 21. Reveille. The storm had passed. We took down our tents and had breakfast. The long hike back to OCS started as soon as we broke camp.

We had gone on other humps, but this was the roughest. We would be marching over mountainous terrain, and many of us were still sick. My cold had settled in my chest, making it difficult to breathe. By now my hacking coughs produced dark phlegm with spots of blood, which I spit on the side of the trail. Fortunately, the sun had come out. The sky was blue. We marched two abreast, one platoon behind another. Although it was still muddy, sections of the trail were covered with dry brown leaves, which cushioned our steps. We all developed blisters, so periodically we were ordered to rest along the side of the trail, take off our boots, and sprinkle talcum powder on our feet.

Marching uphill, our thighs would tighten as we approached the top. Once at the top gravity would help us down the other side, giving our cramping thighs relief. But the bottom of one hill only meant another hill to climb. It was a constant battle against pain and monotony. To bolster our spirits and to set the cadence, we sang Marine Corps songs, which echoed throughout the forest.

"She's waiting for that young Marine far, far away."

"Far away . . . far away."

"She's waiting for that young Marine far, far away."

70　It really did lift our spirits. Word would come down the line that OCS was over the next hill, but we were always disappointed. My legs were numb. My blisters had become open wounds. My back ached. I was dizzy. What was once beautiful scenery soon went unnoticed. I learned to focus on the heels of the candidate in front of me, one step at a time. I caught myself actually asleep at one point. Incredibly, my legs instinctively kept moving. Just as my body was about to quit, the PT deck came into view. There was a chorus of "Urah." With the glow of the setting sun at our backs, we were beginning to feel like Marines.

Wednesday, March 22. The platoon lined up in the hallway adjacent to the squad bay, and started the morning stretching routine. I sat on the floor and began to stretch my legs, back, and shoulders, following the cadence of the candidate platoon sergeant.

"Yamashita . . . get da hell in here!"

It was Brice. Next to ridiculing me, his favorite pastime was giving me evals. There was no way that Brice's treatment of me was constructive. It only served to reinforce the unfair message that I didn't belong. I couldn't understand it. As an African American, he must have understood the harm caused by ethnic slurs and unfair treatment. Yet he engaged in it throughout the course, and through his example, encouraged the same from subordinates.

Sitting behind his desk, he mumbled a question. I hesitated. I knew from experience that whatever my response, it would be wrong.

"What did you say! What did you say!" he thundered. In a rage he reached down, picked up a steel trash can, and threw it at my head. I ducked. It smashed against the wall

Charlie Company, Third Platoon. I am in the front row, third from the right. Front and center are from left to right, Gunnery Sergeant Pitts, Lieutenant Eshelman, and Staff Sergeant Brice, 1989.

behind me, and with a loud bang ricocheted across the floor. On the other side of the wall, the other candidates were still doing their stretching. Vargas told me later that everyone looked at each other with "thank God it's not me" expressions. He conceded that he could not help but think that it was finally going to happen: Brice was going to kill me.

I stood at attention. He screamed for what seemed like an eternity. Then, silence. Suddenly, his demeanor changed.

"You thought I was actually going to hit you, Yamashitow?" he said with a chuckle.

It was as though a completely different Brice was talking. He was calm and collected. His expression said, "I had you going there, didn't I?" Was Brice just testing my mettle? Or was he really out to get me? The answer, though, really didn't matter, for his conduct was poisoning the atmosphere at OCS. I returned to the hallway to join the platoon. I sat down on the floor and continued my stretching. The other candidates looked straight ahead, as if to deny that anything extraordinary had happened.

As I prepared for scheduled exercises in the field that afternoon, I reflected on the candidate billet evaluation. It was yet another aspect of OCS that seemed to be suspect. Billet assignments give the candidate experience in handling different jobs within the company. The billets were rotated among the candidates every two or three days. There were no formal job descriptions. ECPs were the first to be assigned a billet, setting the example for the rest of us.

I reflected on, in particular, my company first sergeant billet. I assumed the duties of the senior enlisted personnel for the company: Master Sergeant Runyun. My performance was not perfect. There were mistakes. But there were no serious mishaps and company business was completed. I expected criticism, but hoped for a balanced and fair review. Instead, I received Runyun's wrath.

> *Absolutely unsatisfactory in all areas: Personal appearance was continuously unkempt, consistently unorganized: never had accurate accountability; unable to complete even minor tasks; lack self confidence, bearing, enthusiasm and initiative. Cannot positively impress others to cause willing obedience to his wishes. Misplaced at OCS.*

It was a disappointment, but I began sensing a disturbing pattern. Two weeks earlier I had been assigned the platoon commander billet. I had taken the platoon out on a conditioning hike, and brought them back without incident. Informally, other candidates had told me that I had done a good job. I wasn't perfect, but as far as I could see, my performance was satisfactory. Yet the evaluation from Lieutenant Eshelman was scathing. Yes, they were the experts telling me that I was no good. But considering how I, and others, had performed, the overwhelmingly negative evaluations seemed off base—and possibly predetermined.

At OCS, pugil sticks is an event not assigned a weight in grading, but can be considered in determining the command evaluation. It is an event simulating close combat

72

where the candidate uses bayonet fighting techniques. I often found myself practicing with Candidate Pugh, as we were about the same height and weight. He was an ECP with lots of practical experience. We were not buddies, but for whatever reason, a mutual respect developed. In the final event, Pugh and I ended up on the same team. When it was my turn, I could hear him shouting encouragement. After I won my match, he sought me out to congratulate me. After all that I was going through, and how desperate I was for a sign of encouragement, it felt good that someone was finally pulling for me.

Later that day we spent the afternoon in the field. Our cammies were covered with dirt and sweat.

"Yamashitee . . . your blouse is not buttoned," yelled Brice.

I looked down at my left breast pocket and buttoned it up. Of course, others had buttons that had come undone. But as always, Brice targeted me. "When you get back to the squad bay, come get your eval form, Yamashitee."

I reported to the duty hut. Brice was sitting behind his desk.

"Here's your eval . . . sign and return it."

I knew the routine. I took the form and began to exit.

"Yamashitee . . . here's another eval, and do you know what this is for?"

"No, Sergeant Instructor," I said, a little confused.

"Because when I ordered you to button your blouse out in the field . . . you didn't!"

"But Candidate Yamashita did button it, Sergeant Instructor," I said with a hint of exasperation.

"Why do you lie to me! Why do you lie to me!"

I stood there at attention.

"Yamashitee, here's another eval form and do you know what this is for?

I didn't answer.

"INTEGRITY VIOLATION!"

This was Brice at his best. It was becoming difficult to take it seriously anymore. Things had degenerated into little more than a petty schoolyard game. I returned to the squad bay and began squaring away my foot locker. Most of the other candidates were still in the showers.

74 "VARGAS! Get your ass in here!" screamed Brice.

I was relieved that it wasn't me this time. As graduation approached, Brice began to pile on the evals. For the moment, Vargas was Brice's new target. His hair still dripping and a towel around his waist, he ran into the duty hut.

"Goddamn it, don't come in here in a towel!" Brice screamed and gave him an eval form.

Vargas returned to the shower room. I knew what was coming next. Watching, I felt like a spectator of my own fate.

"Vargas, get your ass in here!"

Vargas dried his hair and raced to the duty hut. But this time Brice yelled at him for taking so long, which meant another eval. Moments later, Brice called Vargas and gave him yet another form. There was no way for Vargas to escape. I remembered Brice's boast that he could make "anybody look bad."

That week Brice and the others gave me a dozen evals. I sat on my rack intently organizing all my forms. I was startled by a voice from behind. "Gee, if they're going to give you so many evals, then they should at least give you a secretary."

It was Pugh. He was smiling in commiseration. Despite it all, I had to smile back.

Thursday, March 23. I was ordered to report to the seventh week review board. I entered Major Winter's office. He was sitting at the desk surrounded by Mortenson, Eshelman, and Runyun.

"Do you wanna quit?"

"No, Sir!"

"Are you being treated fairly?"

"Yes, Sir!"

Major Winter kept me on probation. As I walked up the stairwell to the squad bay, I steeled myself for the final two weeks. A part of me was still convinced that it was all a test of my mettle. All I needed to do was to have a strong finish. I don't know if it was misplaced optimism, or a refusal to see the writing on the wall, but I felt that I would soon be an officer of Marines.

10

"I Guess the Sun Is Still Shining"

My optimism sprang from experience. In the summer of 1978, while still a student at the University of Hawaii, I was elected one of 102 delegates to the Hawaii State Constitutional Convention.

The year before, the University of Hawaii (UH), in anticipation of the convention, offered a class called "Simulated Constitutional Convention." It looked interesting, but more important, it promised to be an easy course. In class we argued the issues: initiative and referendum, single-member districts, Judicial Selection Commission, unicameral legislature, State Ethics Commission, and Office of Hawaiian Affairs. Toward the end the professor urged students to campaign for the real Constitutional Convention. Margaret thought it was a good idea. I decided to run.

It was a long shot. There were twelve candidates running for the two seats in my district. My campaign committee consisted of Margaret, who became the chairperson, and my cousin Scott, a student at the UH. We had no experience, and jokingly called ourselves the "Triumvirate."

The unthinkable happened. On election night I was elected one of two delegates from my district. To celebrate, Scott and I went fishing on Maui. Little did I know that the other delegates were already scrambling for position. The

My parents with the "Triumvirate" on election night, 1978.

election was nonpartisan, so the convention was being organized into the so-called majority and the independents.

The majority which would control the vote would be a coalition between the "old guard" Democratic Party establishment, and the "young turks," recent graduates of the University of Hawaii Law School. The old guard represented the generation that toppled the Republican Party from power and replaced it with a Democratic machine that would dominate state politics. They remembered a time when Asians were not allowed in the political arena; now they ran the place. Their goal was to maintain the status quo and protect what they had achieved over the years. Although many active politicians shied away from the convention, there were still familiar names: State Senator and Senate Majority Leader Donald Ching and State Senator Robert Taira.

The young turks were mostly recent graduates from the UH law school, and essentially the children of the nisei. There were several delegates that made up the core of the group, but I would have the most contact with John Waiheʻe, Tom Okamura, and Carol Fukunaga. They were proud of local culture, but this was not limited to Hawaii-style mixed plate lunches and *obon* festivals. They brought to the convention a 1960s-style activism and pride in Hawaii's multiethnic community. They were keenly aware of the social injustices of the past, distrustful of mainland influences, and determined to "keep Hawaii, Hawaii." They spoke about helping Native Hawaiians, protecting the environment, and preserving the "aloha spirit."

The independents were the loyal opposition and did their best to keep the majority's feet to the fire. It was made up of delegates not associated with the establishment either politically or socially. Their agenda was to limit the Democratic establishment's ability to wield and hold on to power. I would admire their tenacity as they argued passionately day in and day out, only to lose.

At the convention, I met Kathy Sasaki, a student at the UH who was working for one of the delegates. She was a "country girl" from the island of Kauai and lived at the UH dormitory just down the hill from our house. We began to carpool to the convention. She was attractive, unconventional, and a little eccentric. Usually I made the girls laugh; Kathy made me laugh. Although we spent time together, she had a boyfriend and made it clear that we could only be friends. But as luck would have it, they broke up. We went to the movies. We went fishing and played basketball. She even dragged me to church. She and Margaret became friends. Even my mother liked her! She became my first real girlfriend. But she was more than that: she was my best friend. She was like Marilyn Monroe and Mother Theresa all rolled into one. We are made up of bits and pieces of all those who have come in and out of our lives. To this day, I can still hear her constant reminder that we must "build bridges, not walls."

But as we all know, first loves rarely last. Two years later,

Kathy decided to attend graduate school in the Midwest, so I traveled with her as far as California. I still remember our excitement, as it would be her first trip to the mainland. We flew into Los Angeles and drove to San Francisco. We crossed a desert in the blinding heat; we drove along treacherous cliffs through dense fog; we ate popcorn for dinner to save money.

Before we knew it, we had safely made it to the San Francisco International Airport. Our young lives were spinning off in different directions. All morning we made light conversation, avoiding the thought of parting. We promised that we would stay in touch, but something told me that it was over. Kathy started to cry. And so did I. Even after she disappeared down the ramp, I lingered at the gate until her plane took off. I watched it grow smaller and smaller as it faded into the distance, then out of sight. There's nothing like being young and in love. Now, with each passing year, I look back on those days with increasing gratitude, humility, and wonder.

At the Constitutional Convention, I joined the majority faction, and for the most part toed the party line. My biggest challenge arose over an attempt to take politics out of the selection of Hawaii's judges. Since statehood, the governor had full discretion to make judicial appointments for the Circuit and Supreme Courts. Now, the Committee on the Judiciary recommended creating a nonpartisan Judicial Selection Commission. The commission would take away the governor's discretionary power by presenting a list of judicial candidates from which he or she had to make an appointment. Although the proposal was a good first step, I felt that the objective of eliminating politics had been circumvented in the fine print.

John Waihe'e led a majority caucus seeking the approval of the proposal as it stood. Waihe'e, who was the leader of the young turks, had become the de facto leader of the entire majority. He had it all: education, good looks, political instincts, and charisma. Moreover, he was Native

Hawaiian, a member of a racial group that had largely been left behind socioeconomically. This was the decade when Native Hawaiians had begun to rekindle pride in their culture and assert their sovereign rights. Everyone nodded their heads in agreement. Waiheʻe looked at me. He was a rising political star. I could not help but nod.

But in the end, I couldn't accept the current proposal. I soon found myself lobbying the majority to create a commission that was truly nonpartisan: improvement of the method of Senate confirmation, limit on the number of terms, and a ban on political activity for commission members. I spoke with Walter Ikeda, chairman of the Committee on the Judiciary. There was pressure on him to support the proposal as it stood. But he convinced the majority to support those changes. I was satisfied and moved on to other concerns.

But a few days later, the majority inexplicably withdrew their support for the provision that would ban political activity for commission members. But as a concession, they agreed that I could make my own amendment on the floor of the convention. But without majority support, I knew the likelihood of passage would be nil. Nevertheless, I submitted a written amendment, and prepared my arguments for my floor speech. I conferred with the independents, and lobbied majority members not closely associated with either the young turks or the old guard.

The day of the vote, I got into the office early. I got a surprise call from Walter notifying me of a meeting with the majority leadership. As I entered the president's office, Tom Okamura gave me a cold stare. Senator Ching seemed particularly annoyed. Waiheʻe announced my intention to propose an amendment that would ban political activity for Judicial Commission members. Immediately, it came under attack.

"I think it is going to clutter up our Constitution with provisions that should be handled in the Rules of the Commission," argued Ching.

"This amendment is unnecessary; it could easily be handled by statutes," echoed Delegate Taira.

I argued that they could not assure me that the legislature would have the political will, or the commission members the discipline, to impose such restrictions.

"Shall we withdraw the amendment?" asked John Waihe'e, cutting me off.

I felt betrayed. They had given their approval for me to at least present my amendment on the floor. It was becoming clear that although they believed it had little chance of passage, they were afraid that if they let me propose an amendment on the floor, it would open the floodgates for others to do the same. Before I knew it, a vote to withdraw the amendment had been taken. The rest of the leadership looked on.

"Well, Bruce, that's the decision of the group. Will you now withdraw your amendment?" pressed Waihe'e.

There was silence. I hesitated, and searched Walter's face for an answer. After all, I was just a kid. The leadership was made up of lawyers, legislators, and influential members of Hawaii's Democratic Party. I considered the help that they could provide if I ever wanted to run for another political office, or merely get a job. I slowly nodded my head, and the room seemed to let out a sigh of relief.

Walter and I walked slowly back to our offices. As we neared the elevators on the second floor, I paused and leaned on the railing. The president of the Hawaii Bar Association came running down the hall with my amendment in his hand, and gave me words of support. Embarrassed, I didn't respond. I returned to the office. The results of the meeting had begun to spread.

"Are you going to withdraw the amendment?" demanded a few members of the independents as they charged into my office implying that I was a traitor.

I took a walk around the building to escape the phone calls that were now pouring in. On my way back, I ran into

Carol Fukunaga, who had been at the morning meeting. She tried to reassure me. "It's for the group, Bruce. Sometimes you have to sacrifice."

I went back to the office to prepare for the afternoon session. Baron Gushiken, my administrative assistant, was waiting. I had hired him for his knowledge of legislative procedure. I soon realized that I had gotten much more: researcher, speech writer, strategist, and friend. Baron was a dedicated worker. The office became his second home. Sometimes I would drop by the office after hours, and he would be either organizing files or just playing his guitar. He was the sort of person that would give the shirt off his back to someone in need. He was an idealistic dreamer, a bit stubborn and sometimes impractical. He would always urge me, in subtle and sometimes not so subtle ways, to do the right thing rather than just the smart thing.

Before I knew it Baron and I were discussing the unthinkable: renege on my assurance to withdraw, and propose the amendment on the floor of the convention. Just the thought made me feel like a rat. The discussion went round and round with no resolution.

"Sometimes you have to take a stand," Baron said encouragingly as I left the office.

As I walked onto the convention floor, I was still undecided. There was a large pile of notes on my desk from delegates on both sides of the issue. I knew that some delegates who pledged their support would change their vote if they determined that I was leading a lost cause. I looked over at Walter. I couldn't even count on his vote. I finally called John Waihe'e, and pulled him into a corner.

"I'm telling you, it can be taken care of in the rules!" he yelled. He was physically imposing, and I thought he was going to kick the shit out of me right then and there. But my decision had been made. He glared at me and stomped off.

Sure enough, I felt like a rat. The convention was called

to order. I rose from my seat, avoiding the eyes of the majority members. I tried to speak firmly and slowly.

Today is not an easy day for me. I am proposing this amendment in the face of tremendous opposition. But this morning I looked out the window and realized that the sky is still blue; the people are still going to work; and the sun is still shining. This gives me the strength to do what I believe is right. I am not afraid to speak for what some believe to be a lost cause because I will not be the loser here. I feel that many of us will lose because we bypassed our conscience to vote in favor of a deceptive merit selection process that is more partisan than practical, and more obvious in its intent than objective in its process. This is an important decision for me, for I have definitely crossed the line to clear my conscience. We are not merely shaping a Constitution for temporary convenience, perhaps even anticipating changes in the personality of our governing officers . . . we are dealing with a document of important political, social and historical significance.

Waihe'e argued passionately against it, followed by Delegate Taira. The leadership had spoken, and that was the death knell of my amendment. The members of the majority, as they had done all summer long, began to fall into line. Despite my defiant speech, I began to slump in my chair with visions of having to leave the islands and never coming back.

But then there was a surprise. Thomas Hamilton spoke in favor. It was a spark of hope. Then Jackson Kojima spoke in favor. They were respected members of the majority, but not considered close to either the young turks or the old guard. I sat up in my chair. Walter broke rank. My heart started to beat a little faster. What followed was heated debate that lasted into the afternoon. I tried my best to ward off the attacks. Having run out of arguments, I don't know what I was thinking when I concluded: "as my mother always told me; if there's anything worth doing, it's worth doing well." Looking back I couldn't believe I had said something so stupid. But it brought out a chuckle that rippled across the convention floor—a good way to end an otherwise bitter debate.

There was a roll call vote. Baron passed me an alphabetical list of the delegates. The first few minutes didn't look good. The majority had a comfortable lead. But miraculously, halfway through the vote, it had become neck and neck.

"Oh, shit," whispered Tom Okamura, who was seated next to me.

Several others broke rank. As the clerk began to poll delegates at end of the alphabet, it was clear that it would be close.

"Congratulations, Delegate Yamashita. I guess the sun is still shining," quipped Bill Paty, president of the convention, from the podium.

I leaned back in my chair in disbelief, not quite fully realizing that the amendment had passed. President Paty slammed his gavel, demanding order in the audience and on the convention floor. He too had broken rank.

Delegate Taira rose from his seat and said with a mischievous smile. "And who said we controlled all the votes!"

There was pandemonium on the floor. I was getting ready to sneak out the back door. But as I turned in my chair I came face to face with John Waihe'e, Tom Okamura, and Carol Fukunaga. For a moment I froze, until I realized that they wanted to be the first to congratulate me.

The 1978 Constitutional Convention would have a wide-ranging impact. Despite predictions of moderate reforms, the convention would make changes to the Constitution that would have a huge impact on Hawaii. Delegates would influence politics for years to come. John Waihe'e became governor. Carol Fukunaga became a state Senator. Tom Okamura would become majority leader of the state House. Walter Ikeda became a district court judge. Other delegates would become speaker of the House and the mayor of Honolulu. The members of the old guard, like all good politicians just faded away, but not without leaving an indelible mark on Hawaii. For me, the convention reinforced my belief in the system and the value of keeping the faith despite impossible odds.

11

Destined to Fail

Monday, March 27. Over the weekend, Candidate Wright, my rackmate, had wanted to DOR (Drop on Request), which meant to quit. As I had passed the duty hut I saw Lieutenant Eshelman trying to convince him to stay. That evening Candidate Wright's mattress had been folded and his locker emptied. I could not help but find Eshelman's conduct troubling. Why would he want to keep a candidate that didn't want to be a Marine? Why would the staff bend over backward to help certain candidates, and do everything they could to undermine others? A part of me was still convinced that it was all a test of my mettle. But I could not ignore the unthinkable: the staff had decided who they felt was officer material, and I was not one of them.

But I had to put it out of my mind. It was crunch time. I had been passing all academic requirements with high scores. In physical fitness I wasn't the leader of the pack, but I wasn't "Tail-End Charley" either. In the area of leadership I had passed SULE I, impromptu speech, and the reaction course. But there were two weeks to go, and crucial events lay ahead.

This was the day for the combat conditioning course, which requires completing a 120-yard fireman's carry, 160-yard fire and maneuver course, 3-mile run, 20-foot rope climb, and 30 push-ups. Fail one event and fail the entire course. I passed the first three. The fourth was the rope climb. It required the candidate to scramble up the rope in 30 seconds or less. I was worried, for I had problems with it in practice sessions. Brice held the stopwatch. I ran up and jumped as high as I could. I pulled myself up, hand over hand. I finally reached the top, slapped the log, and screamed "Urah!" I anxiously looked down at Brice.

"Thirty-one seconds," he said without emotion and walked away.

According to Brice's watch, I had failed by one second. This meant I would fail the entire event. After all that had happened, I had no faith in Brice's watch. But all I could do was put it behind me and push on.

Wednesday, March 29. I had passed SULE I. But I needed to pass SULE II, crucial in the leadership evaluation. We had to complete a forced march, reaction course, and an exercise in squad leadership. A lieutenant and a sergeant, neither attached to the 140th OCS, gave me scores of 100 and 91 for the forced march and reaction course. I was ecstatic. All I needed to do was pass squad leadership.

We marched to the SULE II course located off Iwo Jima Trail. Each candidate would be graded by a sergeant instructor. About halfway through, the sergeants ordered a break. We sat down near the bottom of a slope. My turn was still to come. I tried to calm myself as I sat on a pile of dry leaves and leaned against a log. There was a warmth in the air, signaling the coming of spring. A sergeant passed out an MRE; I ripped open the brown foil bag, which contained a paste-like stew. I squeezed it onto several white crackers before wolfing them down. I grabbed another foil bag, tore it open, and ate a small piece of chocolate. I washed it all down with a swig of water from my canteen. It was delicious, but not nearly enough to satisfy my hunger.

"Yamashita . . . you're next!"

The evaluator looked familiar, a sergeant from one of the other platoons. He was carrying the grading sheet and a pen. I jumped to my feet and took a deep breath. The tension I felt was broken by a shrill shout.

"No . . . no . . . no . . . I want Yamashita!"

From the trail that ran across the top of the hill I saw Staff Sergeant Hatfield walking down the slope. His boots made an ominous rustling sound as he walked through the dry leaves. He was the instructor who had berated me in the mess hall the first week of training. He looked down at me and ordered me to begin. I hit all the markers and successfully completed the mission. I was not perfect, but certainly good enough to pass. Indeed, as we marched back a number of candidates told me that they thought I had done a good job.

I returned to camp and happened to walk by Brice, Pitts, Carabine, and Wade. They were all hanging out together like a bunch of juvenile delinquents on a street corner. The feeling of a job well done was interrupted by their barrage of harassment. "Hey, Yamashitow, your belt is crooked. You still can't get squared away. When we get back to the squad bay, come get your eval form," yelled Brice.

For 10 minutes, I stood and answered their questions with the obligatory, "Yes, Sergeant Instructor." Suddenly Candidate Moore ran by.

"Good afternoon, gentlemen," he remarked offhandedly.

Wade snapped back, "Hey, do we look like officers?"

Candidate Moore caught himself. "No, Sergeant Instructor," he answered.

One of the first things that had been drummed into us was protocol. The word "gentlemen" was reserved for the officer corps, and was not to be used when addressing enlisted personnel. That Candidate Moore could have made such a basic mistake was surprising. But more disturbing was that no action was taken against him: no lecture, no eval.

The next day, I was notified that Hatfield had failed me, causing me to fail the entire SULE II event. I was demoralized. I could not succeed if the Marine Corps would not let me.

Monday, April 3. There was growing despair among the

candidates on probation. The constant bombardment was taking its toll. I felt a camaraderie with all of them. Dupalo was the only nonminority. He was tall and muscular, but because of a knee injury was on light duty for weeks. Unlike the rest of us, he seemed to take his predicament in stride. I couldn't help but hope that he knew something that we did not. Jefferson was black and an ECP. Short and muscular, he spoke with a southern drawl, and for the most part kept to himself. The cadre teased him because they claimed that before coming to OCS, he had served in the Marine Corps as a cook.

Candidate Webster appeared to have walked off a Marine poster: six feet tall, husky, broad shoulders, brown hair, handsome face. Although he had lost weight, he still couldn't keep up in PT and was consistently "Tail-End Charley." He was convinced that he would soon be given the ax. But in this system of subjective leadership evaluations, Webster had one powerful intangible going for him: Lieutenant Eshelman liked him, even coining an affectionate nickname for him—"The Web Man."

Woolfolk was black and an ECP from the Air Force. He was small in stature, muscular, with a gentle face. But most striking was an air of sophistication that one would not expect from a candidate from the enlisted ranks. I got the sense that he looked down on Brice, Pitts, and Wade, closer than he was to the "streets." He was frustrated, and openly threatening to quit. I was sitting on my rack when he passed by. Without thinking, I grabbed him by the arm.

"Listen, you're not going to DOR! Just give it four more days!"

Yes, there were just four more days of training. As I saw it, we started OCS, and come hell or high water, we were going to finish it.

That afternoon we had our final fitting at the auditorium. With alterations complete, the petite brunette was proudly holding my olive green coat. It fit perfectly.

"Do you know where they're gonna have the graduation?" she asked.

I remembered the first time I had met her, and how it lifted my spirits. Just feeling the coat had made becoming an officer real. I told her that it would be on the parade deck. She promised that the complete outfit would be delivered in a week. Her demeanor seemed to imply that my graduation was a given. After all, why would the Marine Corps let us go through all the fittings if they didn't intend for us graduate? As I returned to the squad bay, I was again convinced that all of this had to be a good-natured test of my mettle. Perhaps things weren't as dire as they appeared. I was overcome with a sense of relief.

Tuesday, April 4. This was the day for the endurance run. Eshelman had been riding me for weeks. I would have to complete the obstacle course, 3-mile run, stamina course, and combat course in 43 minutes. As I waited, I thought about my failing score of 43:26. The first event was the obstacle course. I had passed this course during the seventh week, but I couldn't forget my earlier failure and injury. We placed our M-16s and cartridge belts with full canteens at the end of the course and jogged back to the start line. Major Winter passed by.

"Listen, you gotta make it, Yamashita. This is critical!"

"Aye, aye, Sir!"

So much was riding on this one event. But it was scored in black and white; there was nothing subjective about it. I would succeed or fail based only on my performance, not on the "opinion" of the staff. I would either run the course in under 43 minutes, or I would not. As I lined up in front of the initial high bar, it started to rain. Now I felt that even the gods were conspiring against me. I looked up at the bar where I had injured my shoulder weeks earlier.

"Yamashita . . . you gotta pass this thing!" yelled Eshelman.

"Aye, aye, Sir!" I screamed at the top of my lungs.

I easily completed the preliminary obstacles. I then ran toward the initial log. I hesitated a moment, then took a deep breath to collect my physical and emotional strength. I bent my knees and jumped into the air, arms upraised. I hit the high bar then swung onto the hand-over-hand pipe. The log walk and the balance log followed. I felt a rush of adrenaline. I raced toward the next series of obstacles. I landed on my feet and headed for the final obstacle: the rope climb. I had had trouble with this particular obstacle before. But practice and watching Candidate Pugh had taught me not to depend solely on upper body strength. The trick was to gain leverage by wrapping the rope between my legs and boots, and then pushing up. This time I made it easily. I slapped the log at the top of the 20-foot rope and screamed, "URAH!"

I threw on my gear, grabbed the M-16, and started the grueling 3-mile run. But I was suddenly overcome with fatigue. I waited desperately for a second wind. My M-16 was getting heavy. The two canteens were banging against my hips. My feet grew heavier as the mud began sticking to the bottom of my boots. The stronger candidates raced ahead. Suddenly I noticed Major Winter, who had decided to jog along the route. He came up behind me. His arms were outstretched like wings, and, instead of words of encouragement, he mockingly swooped toward me, making the sound of an airplane. Before I knew it, he had raced ahead. I used the rhythmic sound of my breathing as a cadence to keep me going: inhale, exhale, inhale, exhale.

I entered the stamina course near Chopawamsic Creek. I crawled face down, dragging my rifle and canteens under a canopy of barbed wire a foot and a half off the ground. I felt a stab of pain as a protruding wire caught my right cammy sleeve, causing a gash on my arm. I desperately worked it free. My arms felt like concrete, but I got through. After the cargo net, I was gasping for air. It would be a mile or so to the combat course.

"C'mon, Candidate Yamashita . . . you can do it . . . I know you can do it!"

It was the Royal Marine who was running alongside me. After a few hundred feet he raced ahead, urging other candidates on the trail. By now my M-16 was draped over my shoulder. The combat course finally came into view.

I made it through the first two obstacles, and then jumped into the quigley. I made my way through the chest-high water, which fed into a concrete tunnel. I lifted my weapon above my head and entered. It was pitch black except for a half circle of light that signaled the other end 20 feet away. By now the water was up to my chin. My mind flashed back to the time when Sergeant Wade had ordered me to do the quigley again. But this time, there was no one around. I was running out of time. I could hear myself grunting as I climbed out of the water and sloshed through the mud.

Now another series of obstacles, this time moving uphill. I knew I was closing in on 43 minutes, and that it was going to be close. I had a sharp pain in my side. My chest hurt. I would either make it, or they would carry me out. I reached the top of the hill. My boots, cammies, weapon, face, hair, and teeth were covered with mud. There was blood all over my sleeve. I came down the hill, jumped into the ford, and, with a last burst of energy, let out a primal scream. I could feel the pull of the water against my legs as I made my way across the dark body of water to the bank at the other side. I dragged myself out, soaking wet. The last 20 yards uphill to the finish line seemed like an eternity. Eshelman was standing there with a stop watch.

"40:00 . . . 40:01 . . . 02 . . . 03 . . . 04 . . . 05 . . ."

Everything was moving in slow motion.

"40:06 . . ." as I crossed the finish.

I bent over gasping for air as I tried to keep walking in a circle. There standing before me was Lieutenant Eshelman with a smile on his face befitting a proud father. He was the

one that had told me that I had to pass, and I had met his
challenge. I had proven that I had the mettle to be a Marine.
As he gave me a bear hug, he shouted in my ear, "Urah!"
Eshelman had been rooting for me from the start. I was
cold, exhausted, and bloodied, but it didn't matter. Instead,
tears of pride welled up; my perseverance and optimism had
paid off. My undying faith in him and the integrity of the
Corps had not been misplaced. As I headed back to the
squad bay, I could still hear in the distance his shouts that
echoed across the field:

"Welcome aboard, Marine!"

The pain and the freezing cold snapped me back to reality. I looked at Lieutenant Eshelman, expecting a word of
congratulations. But he stared straight at me, turned, and
walked away. Still gasping, I saw his disappointment. He
had wanted me to fail. And at that moment, the reality of
the past nine weeks came crashing down on me. I had won
the latest battle, but the war was hopelessly lost. I saw the
disgust and contempt he held for me, and realized that I was
doomed.

Although I didn't know it at the time, I was slowly having to accept what I had ignored for years: that discrimination is real. At Georgetown University I had studied
landmark civil rights cases. I had interacted with minority
students clamoring for justice. But it had always been
abstract. It had always been difficult for me to relate. It had
always been someone else's battle.

12

"Too Many JAPS around Here"

THE GEORGETOWN UNIVERSITY LAW CENTER IS NOT on the main campus, but across town on Capitol Hill near Congress, Judiciary Square, and the U.S. Supreme Court. After my first class, I followed the horde down to the cafeteria in the basement. I grabbed some pizza and found an open seat. An attractive woman with reddish-brown hair sat across from me.

"So, how do you like Georgetown?" I smiled, trying to make light conversation.

She leaned over as if to share a secret. "Too many JAPS around here," she said.

I blanched, convinced that I misunderstood. She continued, nonplussed.

"You know. Jewish American Princesses," she whispered.

I nodded as if I understood. In Honolulu we have one Jewish temple. We know one Jewish family, Melvin and Thelma Ezer and their three sons. Over the years, I had gone to their respective bar mitzvahs. But I had not heard of a Jewish American Princess before.

My parents had wanted me to go to law school right after college, but instead I chose to live and work abroad. Four years in Japan had taught me much about the world and myself. But I was getting older, and so were my parents. After Margaret had gotten her Ph.D. and Allen his MBA,

there was parental pressure to pursue some sort of graduate degree right away. Most of my dad's scrimping and sav-
ing went toward educating his children, and he wanted to
put tuition worries behind him.

My initial excitement about law school soon gave way
to grade grubbing and competition. Compared to my   **95**
classmates, I felt like an intellectual pipsqueak. I hated it.
But there were memorable opportunities to learn. My constitutional law professor, Peter Edelman, had assigned *Roe
v. Wade*, the case legalizing abortion. The twenty of us in
the class began to discuss the case, when Professor Edelman
offhandedly offered a suggestion. Perhaps, he said, we
would like to discuss *Roe* with the Supreme Court justice
who authored this landmark decision. Professor Edelman's
younger brother had served as Justice Harry Blackmun's
first law clerk. So we walked over to the U.S. Supreme
Court and into Justice Blackmun's chambers, and amidst
the splendor of the nation's highest court, class resumed.

While one journey of self-discovery had ended, another
had just begun. While Japan allowed me to discover my
roots, law school forced me to broaden my understanding
of America. Washington in the mid-1980s was largely a
black and white society. For the first time in my life, I felt
conspicuous. I would enter a restaurant and be the only
Asian there. Clerks would ask me where I learned my English; kids on the corner of Dupont Circle would give me a
kung fu chop as I passed; businessmen assumed that I
worked at one of the embassies. At first it was humorous,
but soon it became irritating. In Japan, even though I
looked Japanese, my language, attitude, and mannerisms
would give me away as an American. But in Washington,
even though I spoke native English and felt very American,
there were those who saw only my Asian face.

Life outside law school was almost nonexistent. After class
on Fridays, I'd head for the gym on the main campus with
a few classmates for pick-up basketball games. Afterward,

we would go for pizza and beer, but even the drinking was not like it was in Japan. One or two beers and we would call it a night.

On one occasion we went into Georgetown. M Street was crowded with undergrads starting out the weekend. Several of us aspiring lawyers huddled together, arguing about where to go. My hands freezing, I impatiently moved off to the side, remarking, "Would you guys hurry up!"

"Hey, hold your horses, TOJO!" a voice shot back.

That could only have come from Greg Slone. Sometimes Greg would approach me in the library and quietly sing the 1960s song "Secret Agent Man," but replace those lyrics with "Secret Asian Man." On other occasions he would come up to me bowing, "Hai Wakarimasu, Toranaga sama," which he claimed he memorized from the movie *Shogun*. But I took it in stride. Greg was not an instructor. He was not a stranger. He was a friend. I could always tell him to go to hell—and on a few occasions, I did.

In Hawaii, I was used to this sort of ribbing. Comedians make their living off ethnic jokes, based on local stereotypes. Mainlanders often are offended. Understanding the history of racial violence on the mainland, I don't blame them. But what they fail to appreciate is that for Hawaii the sugar plantation experience is far more relevant than slavery. It is not white versus black, but a multitude of groups that had to live together. These jokes are not meant to denigrate, but instead recognize that each group has, and continues to make, a unique contribution to our multiethnic, multicultural community. Sad will be the day when even in Hawaii we can no longer celebrate our diversity by poking fun at each other . . . and at ourselves.

I joined the Asian Pacific American Law Students Association (APALSA). I attended the seminars on substantive issues: affirmative action, immigration policy, negative Asian images in the media, language rights, and hate crimes. But while these issues interested students from the mainland, I couldn't see the relevance to me. After all, I was in law school, didn't speak with an accent, and came from a solid middle-class background.

One morning before class I told a classmate that I didn't see the necessity for affirmative action. She had cornered me about the difficulties women and minorities faced in the legal profession, in first getting in the door at a major law firm, then breaking into the white-male-dominated ranks of partners. She thought she'd find an ally in me. She continued to push the issue.

"I don't know why everyone's always complaining," was my response. "My grandfather came to this country and had nothing, and he made it. Why can't everyone else?"

To this day, I remember the look on her face, a look of sheer disbelief. I think that if I were white instead of Asian, she would have punched me. Truth be told, it wasn't that I was against affirmative action; it's just that I hadn't given the issue much thought. The irony is that looking back objectively, the only reason I was at Georgetown probably had to do with affirmative action. Although my grades were high, my scores on the LSAT, the standardized qualifying exam, were less than stellar.

I didn't come to Georgetown to be an activist, anyway. To me, the people who marched in the 1960s, although admittedly heroic, had little to do with me. That female student, the Asian Pacific American Law Students Association, all of them should learn to relax. The real reason I joined APALSA, anyway, was social: the opportunity to hang out with other Asian/Pacific students, particularly those from Hawaii.

To that end, I became the group's social chair, and decided to throw a bash for members from all the Washington-area law schools. I handled everything, even going around to American University, Catholic University, and George Washington University to tack up the posters I had made for the event. Though hardly an artist, I was proud of my work, which headlined what I thought would be "can't miss" attractions:

"Free Booze. Ono Food. Wild Women."

The last of the posters nailed up, I headed home, satisfied with a job well done. Then, all hell broke loose.

In a decade of political correctness, I had failed the sensitivity test miserably. Women law students of Asian descent flooded the Georgetown Law School administration with calls of complaint. Who, they demanded to know, was responsible for this "wild women" poster, the one that played to the worst stereotypes of Asian women as "Suzie Wongs," "geisha girls," and "boy-toys"?

When I was called into the office of the dean, I didn't understand. What, I asked, was wrong? The phrase was intended as nothing more than an expression of red-blooded American masculinity to get people to come to a party. Why, I wondered, were all these women upset? Couldn't they take a joke?

They, of course, had the last laugh. They organized a boycott of my party that spread to their male colleagues. My debut as social chair ended up a disaster. I spent that night with a couple of the guys from Hawaii. We were surrounded by food, and downed the free booze in a futile attempt to put the party out of our minds.

Inevitably, I would again pay the price for my ignorance and disinterest. During a class in constitutional law taught by Professor Francis Drinan, the assignment was to recite the facts and holdings of *Korematsu v. United States*. I studied as I usually did: 15 minutes skimming the facts and memorizing the holding. After the attack on Pearl Harbor, 120,000 citizens and aliens of Japanese ancestry were deemed "security risks." They were forced from their homes and placed in internment camps. Fred Korematsu, a nisei welder in Oakland, refused to obey the evacuation orders and was arrested, convicted, and sent to a relocation camp. In 1943, the United States Supreme Court ruled that the government had not violated his constitutional rights: the evacuation orders were justified by the war as "proper security measures."

Forty years later, in conjunction with the political movement for reparations, a group of sansei lawyers filed a petition to reopen the Korematsu case. In 1983, a United States District Court, based on new information that officials had altered, suppressed, and destroyed evidence, held that the government had violated Korematsu's constitutional rights.

But that morning, my only concern was whether I would be called on. I had participated in class the week before, so the way I saw it, I was in the clear.

"Today is *Korematsu v. United States*. It's a case of injustice against a Japanese American," Professor Drinan announced, sweeping the room with his eyes, pausing to look at me momentarily. I sank in my chair and tried to avoid eye contact. Out of 120 students, there were two Asians.

"Mr. Yamashita," he boomed, walking straight toward me.

Of course he would pick me. I had barely done the reading and had nothing to say. I had that sinking feeling that all law students experience at one time or another. I am embarrassed to say that as a Japanese American I had not heard of Korematsu before reading the case, nor did I realize its landmark nature. The internment was something that happened to people from another time, and the struggle for reparations had little direct bearing on my life. I could tell that Professor Drinan wanted more than just the facts. He expected personal history, insight, passion. All eyes were upon me. But I had no insight to offer. Stalling for time, I mumbled something about an injustice.

"But why was it an injustice?" he thundered.

I looked down and fumbled through a few more pages. Hands shot up around me. Mercifully, Professor Drinan turned to others for the answer. As I sat in class only half-

Fred Korematsu and I at a reception in San Francisco, 1994.

listening to the discussion, the thought came to me that my embarrassment didn't rise from being caught unprepared. That had happened before, and it would happen again. It was because I was unprepared for a case that should have had profound personal meaning.

Years later I had the honor of meeting Fred Korematsu. By then, I knew him for what he was: a hero not only for Japanese Americans, but for all Americans. He had dared to speak out against injustice, no matter what the consequences, at a time when others did not.

As I shook his hand, I could see in my mind's eye a classroom at Georgetown Law School, where a younger man was beginning to discover an America that was far larger and more complex than he had always known.

13

"The Writing on the Wall"

Wednesday, April 5. "Catipon, Dupalo, Jefferson, Vargas, Webster, Woolfolk, and Yamashitee: report to ninth week review board this afternoon," deadpanned Brice.

We spent the day out in the field. About midafternoon, the staff ordered us to report to company headquarters for the review board. We returned to the squad bay and began to change out of our dirty cammies. We had come so far together, and now faced an uncertain fate. For a moment I reflected on the past weekend. Candidate Pugh had invited me to join him and others to party in Georgetown. He had a car, and could give me a ride. A night away from OCS was tempting, but I had decided to stay on base to spit-shine my boots and prepare. I had clung to the hope that if I performed perfectly the final week, everything would turn out fine. My thoughts snapped back to the present as I opened my locker and admired my cleanly pressed cammies. Everyone else had gone down to the review board.

From out of the corner of my eye, I could see Brice quietly sitting at his desk. His abusive conduct had continued until the end. Earlier that week during a class held near the obstacle course, he had thrown me to the ground while others looked on. As I started to change, I noticed that he had gotten up out of his chair.

"Eh, Yamashitee . . . what do you think you're doing"? he said as he exited the duty hut.

"This candidate is changing into clean cammies," I said with pride.

"You leave your dirty cammies on . . .whether you are retained or not has nothing to do with your cammies being clean."

102

I stood there in shock. From the beginning the sergeant instructors had emphasized the importance of being squared away. How many evals had I received for allegedly not having my cammies clean and pressed? Now for the all-important ninth week review board, Brice was telling me not to change!? But orders were orders. I had no time to ponder the motivation behind Brice's latest shenanigan. I changed back into my dirty cammies and boots. I took a place in the line that had formed in the hallway outside company headquarters. Everyone was at attention. I was finally called in.

"How dare you come in with a cammy that's filthy?!" screamed Captain Mortenson, the company executive officer, as he jumped to his feet.

I had a perfectly pressed cammy hanging in my locker. Should I tell them about Brice? I had not complained for nine weeks, and I had no intention of starting now. But I concluded that at this point, I had to at least tell the truth.

"Did he really order that?" asked Major Winter, appearing angry.

I braced myself for further inquiry. Certainly the officer corps would want to know of any improper conduct by their subordinates. But there was no follow-up. There were no questions. Instead, they screamed at me for what seemed like an eternity about my dirty cammy.

The review board was a disaster. No one had anything good to say. Eshelman didn't even mention the endurance run. They ordered me "across the street" to go before the final battalion review board.

"I made it!" he shouted.

As I returned to the squad bay, I had bumped into Vargas. They had taken him off probation. A smile spread over my face as I gave him a high-five and a hug. Sure I was envious, and wondered why he should make it and not I. But the weeks of unfair harassment had created a genuine camaraderie, and I felt a sense of vindication that at least one of us would make it.

As I walked toward the head, I passed a candidate from another platoon who asked how it went. I shook my head.

"Well, don't worry. I was talking to second lieutenants at the Basic School, and they pass everyone; they don't drop you once you get this far!"

I marched out of Charlie Company, across the courtyard, and over the footbridge to the field. The order to go "across the street" meant that I was 48 hours from being disenrolled. But my chance meeting in the hall had again lifted my spirits. At this point, I was ready to believe anything.

I joined the rest of the platoon who were out in the field honing their skills on the confidence course. Brice made a beeline for me.

"Did you tell the board I told you to change back into a dirty uniform?"

"Yes, Sergeant Instructor," I said with hesitation.

Brice stared at me. I looked back at him, not knowing what to think. Years later I would appreciate the irony. A common complaint in the civilian world is that Asians are promoted to and kept in low management positions so they can do the firing of African Americans and Latinos, thereby insulating their white employers from discrimination lawsuits. In many ways, the same thing was happening at OCS. But this time, the tables had been turned: Brice was "middle management" who would sabotage my performance, provide ample documentation, and, most important, protect the officer corps. But at that moment as I looked at Brice, I knew none of these things.

Thursday, April 6. Final company inspection. Remembering what the candidate had told me in the squad bay, I still believed that maybe I'd be taken off probation. I spit-shined my boots, pressed my cammies, and cleaned my rifle.

It was a cold, gray afternoon. The wind blew across the Potomac River straight into our faces. Major Winter finally appeared and started the inspection. Out of the corner of my right eye I noticed that he had stopped in front of a candidate. He grabbed the rifle, pulled the bolt, and checked the chamber in one swift action. He moved to the next platoon, stopped in front of a candidate, and asked an odd question about what sort of car he drove.

"A Ford, Sir!" the candidate shouted.

"Good, I'm sure glad you don't drive a JAPANESE car!"

A chill went up my spine. He then made his way straight toward me. There was an eerie pause. He grabbed my weapon, but didn't even look at it.

"This rifle is filthy!"

Even I began to see the writing on the wall. But, I stubbornly refused to accept the inevitable.

14

"Disenrolled!"

Friday, April 7. "Catipon, Dupalo, Jefferson, Vargas, Woolfolk, and Yamashitee report to battalion headquarters for the final review board this afternoon," yelled Gunnery Sergeant Pitts.

The rest of the morning we spent in the field running the final OCS event: the battle fitness test (BFT). As we crossed the finish line a few teams were already celebrating on the parade deck. We had survived! There were hugs and high-fives.

But the elation of surviving OCS was brief. After lunch the staff ordered the six of us to return to the squad bay. The mood became somber. Candidate Webster, who had been "Tail-End Charley" all nine weeks, was suddenly taken off probation. Candidate Vargas was not as fortunate. The staff had placed him back on probation, and ordered him "across the street." Vargas was changing quietly near his rack. He had been on an emotional roller coaster, and it showed.

As I made final preparations, Brice came out of the duty hut.

"So you goin' across the street, Yamashitee," he said quietly as he tugged gently at my cammy sleeve, making sure that it was straight.

"Yes, Sergeant Instructor."

He quickly checked all my buttons to make sure they were secured. "I've been sort of like your dad, haven't I?"

Desperate for even the slightest encouragement, it was a remark that tore at my emotions. "Yes, Sergeant Instructor," I said as my voice cracked.

106   "Just try your best," he said quietly. "Things will be fine."

I ran downstairs and joined the others. We marched across the footbridge over the tracks to battalion headquarters. We sat down on a long bench in front of the barber shop. Sitting there triggered memories of our first haircut. As we sat there in silence, I studied the worried faces of the others. I noticed that five out of six of us were minorities. Indeed, *all* the minority candidates in Third Platoon were going before the colonel.

I could not help but reflect on my encounter with Brice in the squad bay moments earlier. His words of encouragement only reinforced my belief that it had all been a test. If I endured, and didn't quit, then I would graduate. It was the only way to make sense out of the bizarre conduct of the 140th OCS staff: racial harassment, trumped-up evals, and unfair grading. It was the only way to legitimize a seemingly corrupt system. I thought about how Webster had been saved. It didn't make sense; he couldn't run from here to there without getting tired. I thought about Kempster, who had been taken off probation even though he had been on light duty for weeks. I thought about how Vargas had been taken off and then placed back on probation all within 48 hours. It had to be a test! They would let us twist in the wind, some of us longer than others, but in the end they would let us graduate.

A Marine appeared. Dupalo leaped to his feet and disappeared into the hallway. A few enlisted personnel walked into the barbershop giving us sympathetic looks. Dupalo was disenrolled. Vargas was next. He too was kicked out. Ditto for Catipon. I sat there in stunned silence. Jefferson was next. That left only me and Woolfolk.

"Candidate Yamashita!"

I was led down the hallway and ordered to wait in a small room. Jefferson was still before the colonel. Suddenly I heard yelling. My heart started to pound. Then there was a long silence. The door flew open.

"You're next," deadpanned the Marine.

I walked to Reinke's office and centered myself at the hatch.

"Candidate Yamashita, reporting as ordered, Sir!"

I entered the office and came to attention. Colonel Reinke was anchored behind a large desk. He was a Marine's Marine, muscular and distinguished. The walls were covered with certificates, diplomas, and awards. Behind the desk were the American, Marine Corps, and OCS flags. Seated around me were Major Winter, Captain Mortenson, and Lieutenant Eshelman. The only new face was Captain Victor Garcia, the battalion executive officer. Everyone stared at me, eyes cold and expressionless. Eshelman began reading a statement.

"This candidate is still behind the power curve. He has not learned basic military skills. I recommend disenrollment . . ."

He spoke for several minutes. He had nothing positive to say. There was no mention of the endurance run. When Colonel Reinke noted my score of 95 for public speaking, Eshelman responded derisively, "It only shows that he's a good talker."

Reinke asked if I had anything to say for myself.

"To disenroll me now would be a mistake. I have made great progress and . . ."

He cut me off and slammed his gavel.

"Candidate Yamashita, you are disenrolled!"

The emotional roller coaster I had been riding for nine weeks had ended, and I had gone off the cliff. I had given up so much to be here. My hands were sweaty, my mouth was dry, my legs felt like rubber. I stood for the last time as an officer candidate.

"Dismissed!"

"Aye, aye, Sir!"

I took one step backward, made an about face, and started to march out.

"Candidate Yamashita!"

I stopped in my tracks, and turned my head toward the colonel.

"I heard you flunked your bar exam!" said Reinke in a loud voice with a mocking smile. The rest of the staff broke out in laughter.

"Were You Treated Fairly?"

THE WORLD SEEMED TO BE MOVING IN SLOW motion. I left battalion headquarters, oblivious of the blue sky and warm spring sunshine. Making my way across the train tracks, I instinctively looked for Brice, but realized that he no longer mattered. I slumped down on a curb facing Charlie Company. It was a rare moment of solitude. As I gazed out on the Potomac River, my eyes began to well up.

I had been accepted as an officer candidate and assumed that this meant that the United States Marine Corps would give me an equal opportunity to succeed. I believed that in the end my perseverance and improvement would be to my credit. The sense of betrayal came from the humiliating realization that in fact they had never wanted me. They had piled it on in an effort to make me quit, and when I wouldn't quit, they had to kick me out.

Later I would speak with Uncle Daniel about what had happened at OCS. For the first time he explained to me in detail an event that he had been reluctant to speak about. On August 25, 1944, the battle of the Arno River was raging. "I" Company had fought their way northward up the Italian coastline. They were encamped near a farmhouse waiting for orders. Uncle Daniel walked up a slight incline toward the radio man, who was leaning against a tree on a hill. They talked briefly before he turned and walked away. There was a thunderous blast. Enemy mortar fire hit the top of the tree, and sent searing metal shrapnel toward the ground. The fragments struck a nearby ammunition carrier, causing more explosions. The radio man was blown up. Uncle Daniel was hit in the head and back and thrown toward the bottom of the hill. Two weeks later the family received a letter from the adjutant general, War Department, Washington, D.C.: "Regret to inform you, report received states your brother Staff Sergeant Daniel T. Yamashita, was seriously wounded in action 25, August 1944."

I made my way back to the squad bay. I took the pantry entrance to company headquarters. Brice was standing there.

"So what happened?" he asked like an anxious father.

"I was disenrolled," I said in a daze.

"Damn!"

Brice kicked the wall. I stood and watched in disbelief. How long would he keep up the charade? I stood there, waiting for him to give me a sign that it had all been bullshit and that indeed I had been duped. I wanted the real Brice to stand up. I wanted him to admit that all along he had merely been an obedient servant doing the officer corps' dirty work. Instead, he convincingly shook his head in frustration and stomped away.

My mind was racing. Was it possible that Brice had been on my side? That would at least let me escape with an ounce of faith in the system. I allowed myself to ponder whether Brice had actually gone to bat for me as promised, but in the end was simply betrayed by the officers. I allowed myself to believe that he was just as disappointed as I was. His words weeks earlier echoed in my head, "At the end, if I like you, I repeat, IF I LIKE YOU, I'll go talk to Major Winter. And you're gonna graduate. You understand me?"

By now the word had spread that I had been disenrolled along with Catipon, Vargas, Dupalo, and Jefferson. I returned to the squad bay. I passed Wade and Carabine. Gunnery Sergeant Pitts summoned me to the duty hut.

"Get back into the squad bay and clean out your locker," he said in a low voice.

Pitts ordered candidates to help me. The Candidate Regulations which had specified the proper way to store clothing and personal items went out the window. My wall locker flew open, and my foot locker was dragged to the middle of the squad bay. The contents were poured into a duffel bag.

All of us had been through hell together, and whether we liked it or not, a bond had been formed. Cederholm and Wagner came to say good-bye. Pugh shook my hand.

"You're okay, Yamashita. Good luck."

It was time for me to join the dreaded R&S platoon. Pitts ordered Third Platoon on line as he walked down the squad bay.

"We all know that Candidate Yamashitee gave it his all and never quit."

"Urah!" a single voice echoed through the squad bay.

"Urah!" more voices joined in.

"Urah!" this time the whole platoon.

My body began to shake. Tears welled up and flowed down my cheeks. The acknowledgment that I got from those three "Urahs" was what I had expected officially from the Corps. I grabbed my bag, and headed for the stairwell. Brice, still reminding me of a Coke machine, suddenly appeared in front of the duty hut. I paused for a moment. Oddly, now there wasn't a glint of commiseration. I looked at him one last time, desperate for an explanation. But he glowered back at me. It was like time had finally stopped. I turned toward the stairwell and disappeared.

Candidate Dupalo was already waiting in the pantry for transportation to the R&S platoon. He was the only non-minority to be disenrolled from the platoon. I collapsed on my duffel bag, and joined the wait. Amazingly, I was still half expecting somebody to tell me that it had all been a test, and that I would be commissioned after all. I could hear the rest of the candidates whooping it up in celebration. As I sat there, it was almost unbearable.

The doors swung open and Master Sergeant Runyun appeared. There was something in me that desired closure. At the end of a game, win or lose, you go up to your opponent and shake his hand. Maybe it was a little of this that made me approach him.

"Candidate Yamashita requests permission to speak!"

Runyun looked at me with a blank stare. This was the sergeant who had spoken to me in Japanese. This was the sergeant who said that I was misplaced at OCS. There was an uncomfortable silence.

"No!"

He turned sharply and marched away.

A few moments later the pantry doors flew open again. It was Lieutenant Eshelman. He looked down at us with a blank stare and continued on without saying a word. Eshelman was in charge of Third Platoon. Yes, we were disenrolled. We were no longer officer candidates. But we had been under his command for nine weeks.

I expected him to at least look us in the eyes and wish us well. Granted, it may have been awkward, but as I saw it, that's why he was an officer. I was disappointed, but not surprised at his lack of leadership.

Our new quarters were across the tracks in an old dilapidated squad bay, a reminder that we were no longer officer candidates. The others were already there. Woolfolk was saved at the last minute, and would be the lone minority to graduate. Jefferson, Vargas, Dupalo, and I were leadership failures. For Catipon, it was PT. Both he and Webster had struggled with the physical training, and failed the endurance run. But at the ninth week board, the officer corps had decided to allow Webster to retake the run, and I would learn later that he eventually "passed." They had not allowed Catipon to retake the run even though he had a better overall academic and leadership record. Incredibly,

Candidate Kempster came off light duty during the latter half of OCS, was taken off probation, and would be commissioned an officer of Marines.

Disenrolled candidates from First and Second Platoons trickled into the squad bay. Out of a group of eleven, ten were smaller in stature and/or a racial or ethnic minority. I **113** began to wonder whether the OCS command had targeted certain individuals for disenrollment, not just in Third Platoon, but in the entire company. I began to wonder whether racial remarks and unfair treatment had also occurred in the other platoons, creating a similar slippery slope for the unsuspecting victims.

The officer in charge entered the room and without emotion explained the procedures for out-processing. After nine weeks of rules and regulations, I felt lost amidst the freedom. We sat around a recreation room adjacent to the squad bay. There was a small TV, and under any other circumstance, it would have been a treat to relax and catch up with the outside world. But I couldn't watch anything. I couldn't eat. Most of us were still in a state of denial. We weren't really being disenrolled. Someone would come in and order us back to Charlie Company. Heck, our uniforms were fitted and ready for the graduation ceremony.

Saturday, April 8. There was no reveille. Several of us rented a van and drove into Washington, D.C. It was the weekend before the graduation. We had a few beers at Houlihan's on M Street, listened to music, and tried to enjoy ourselves. But it was a futile attempt. We had accepted our disenrollment. Now, we worried about how to tell family and friends. To avoid being maudlin, we resorted to humor. One of the disenrolled candidates from Second Platoon joked that I should turn my efforts toward manufacturing my own automobile.

"Yeah, the YAMASHITA 140Z . . . it may not run that well, but it will never, ever quit."

They all laughed. Even I had to smile. Everyone started

to relax, and for the first time we had a chance to get to know each other.

Monday, April 10. R&S platoon marched to the administration building. But now the line was crooked and our shoulders slumped. We looked like shit, but we didn't care.

We sat down on the bench, waiting for an interview with the chaplain. While we were there the Royal Marine appeared. "What are you doing here?" he asked, surprised to see me.

I sprang to my feet. "I've been disenrolled, Sir."

He rolled his eyes, and then composed himself.

"Listen, you finished and never quit. You've got nothing to be ashamed of, and don't you ever forget that."

Eshelman could have learned much from this Royal Marine about leadership.

Tuesday, April 11. We turned in our uniforms, weapons, and equipment, then marched to battalion headquarters for our final out-processing interview. They told us that this would be our "last chance" to speak to a Marine officer about OCS. Captain Garcia called us in one by one. The interviews lasted about 10 minutes, so the line moved quickly. I marched into the bare office, where Captain Garcia sat behind a desk. A female lieutenant was seated to my right toward the wall. The strict reporting procedures were no longer required.

"Were you treated fairly?"

I thought to myself, Here we go again. The days of the perfunctory, proper response were over. I had not uttered a word of complaint for nine weeks, but I could no longer be silent.

"No, Sir," I responded tersely.

Captain Garcia looked up with surprise from the papers he was reading on his desk. Now I had his attention.

"I didn't appreciate all the derogatory racial remarks directed at me," I continued.

Captain Garcia stared at me. This interview was supposed to be a formality. I had not given him the answer he had expected. He recovered quickly, and said that racial remarks were allowed at OCS. Incredulous, I countered that there was a difference between criticizing a candidate for poor performance and harassing him for his ethnicity. Garcia argued that when he was a candidate, the staff had made racial remarks about his ethnic background. He boasted that it had made him a better Marine. We went back and forth; at times the discussion became heated.

115

Before I left the room I demanded to see my peer evaluations. He promised to provide them before I left Quantico. It would be the first of many broken promises. I didn't know it at the time, but Garcia's conduct and attitude would be a preview of what was to come from the Corps.

Wednesday, April 12. I had one final task. My Service "A" uniform, which had been fitted and refitted, needed to be returned. I slung it over my shoulder and waited outside the squad bay. As I stood there, I ran my fingers over the neatly pressed lapel, and gazed at the anchor and globe button. The vendor drove up and honked his horn, which snapped me out of my thoughts. I ran to the car and saw the petite brunette in the passenger seat. She was dressed casually in jeans and a cotton top. "Well, at least you finished the course," she said in a soft voice.

She smiled uncomfortably, certainly wondering why I had been kicked out. Performance? Integrity? I gently placed the uniform in the back seat. As they drove off, I waved, trying to hide my embarrassment.

I returned to the squad bay for the bus that would take us to the Amtrak train station. To add insult to injury, we could hear Charlie Company practicing on the parade deck for the graduation ceremony on April 14, in 48 hours. Not a word was said as we rumbled passed the battalion headquarters, parade deck, Charlie Company, mess hall, and Larson Gymnasium.

The train left Quantico, headed back to Washington, D.C. I gazed out the window and saw visions of bivouacs, conditioning hikes, obstacle courses, quigleys and endurance runs. I was in the best physical shape of my life. But emotionally I was a wreck. In Japanese there is the word *haji,* or shame. Six months earlier I had flunked my bar exam. And now the Marine Corps had told me I was a reject. I would be returning home branded with that label and the stigma of falling short. I had brought shame upon myself, family, and community. What would I say? What would I do with the rest of my life?

16

First Step, False Hope

1989–1990

Returning home several weeks later, I was still searching for a way to make sense out of the disaster that was OCS. The utter and abject sense of failure remained, but I was convinced I had given it my best shot. There was no choice except to put the Marines behind me and move on.

At the time I was oblivious to any meaning behind the decision to go back to Hawaii. It just seemed like the natural thing to do. Multiethnic Hawaii provided a place that in attitude was the polar opposite of what I had just experienced in Quantico. Instinctively, I was drawn back to a refuge of familiarity, safety, and support.

But I still dreaded my reunion with the family. They were waiting at the airport: Mother, Pop, Margaret, and her kids. They thought they were being supportive.

"Thank God you didn't make it!" Margaret gushed.

"It's God's will. Now it's time to move on," my mother added.

Of course, there were many questions. But I sidestepped them all with obfuscation and feigned indifference. But inside, what felt the worst was the Marine Corps' judgment that I was a leadership failure.

I stalled for a few days before building up the courage to inform Ernie Kimoto that I had been disenrolled. He had recently retired from the Marine Corps and was working at the Hawaii Attorney General's Office. As I walked into his office he still looked like a Marine: stocky and muscular. He had a "high and tight" and still reminded me of a bull terrier. Probably because I felt so embarrassed, I just told him that things hadn't worked out. A man of little emotion, he took the news matter of factly. Perhaps respecting my privacy, he didn't ask for the details. Instead, he asked about my future. I told him that the first step was to pass the bar exam. I thanked him for all his help. Any path now open to me would take me farther and farther from the Marine Corps and Ernie Kimoto.

Spring turned to summer. I spent most of my time preparing again for the Hawaii bar, the rest feeling sorry for myself. When I had first taken the exam I was motivated, anticipating a career as a judge advocate in the Marine Corps. This time, with no goal in sight, it was pure drudgery. When I wasn't in the review course, I was at the University of Hawaii's Sinclair Library. The only person I spent any time with was Baron Gushiken, my former aide at the Constitutional Convention. He made me laugh, and peppered me with questions about the exam. I found that there is no better way to understand the law than to have to explain it a nonlawyer. When I finally took the exam, I felt I had done well. But after the beating my self-confidence had taken, I was prepared for the worst. I did, however, pass, and I could almost hear my family sighing in unison with relief. Most important, it was another concrete step toward putting OCS behind me.

"So what happened with the Marine Corps?" asked Al Goshi, a friend from law school who couldn't have known how critical that off-handed question would turn out to be. We were at a small Georgetown reunion in Honolulu. Al had graduated from West Point, was sent to law school, and now was a captain in the Army JAG Corps. I recounted my experience. Al listened with amazement.

"Well, I don't know about the Marine Corps, but in the Army you don't touch that stuff with a 10-foot pole. It is *verboten* . . . period."

I could feel the anger returning. Days later, I could still hear the echo of those words over and over: "*verboten* . . . period." For the past five months I had convinced myself that, despite the circumstances, only I was to blame for my disenrollment. It was a conclusion that sprang from the generations-old belief of my parents and their parents: the way to overcome obstacles was silence and hard work. But taken to extremes, it became humiliation that sometimes led not to graceful acceptance, but to self-doubt and despair.

The first person I spoke to was Margaret. Of course, after telling her the truth, I was bracing for a resounding, "I told you so!" Instead, she was angry, and believed that I had an obligation to do something. I don't know what I would have done if she had felt that it was a lost cause. In those first few tentative months she became my lone adviser, editor, and coach.

That week I couldn't sleep. I decided to visit the local Marine Corps recruiting station on Kapiolani Boulevard. I had convinced myself that it was just an inquiry. Little did I know that it signified my first challenge to the Marine Corps. Little did I know that it would be the beginning of another journey as painful as OCS itself. Captain Dyer and Captain Rivera were shocked to hear my story, and assured me that what had happened to me was not consistent with Marine Corps policy. I spoke with a Navy recruiting officer who confirmed that making derogatory racial remarks was not tolerated. Everyone I talked to, officially or unofficially, was appalled.

I felt vindicated, and dared to envision myself back in the Corps. I even made a telephone call to a Colonel Slack in Washington. I had met him before entering the 140th OCS, as he had been in charge of personnel matters. I remembered him being particularly helpful and supportive. This time he advised me to keep my grievances "in house" and give the Corps a chance to rectify the situation. At the time the advice seemed reasonable. But that veneer of receptiveness was to become a typical institutional reaction from the Corps. Inevitably, the disarming responses led to inaction and stalling.

But in November 1989, I knew none of this, and I gratefully took Colonel Slack's advice. So more than six months after I had been disenrolled, I began drafting a letter to General Alfred Gray, commandant of the Marine Corps. I explained what had happened at the 140th OCS. I asked for a definitive statement on the Marine Corps' policy on the use of racial remarks. Captain Garcia had said one thing. Others had told me another. I wrote that if my treatment had been contrary to Marine policy, then my disenrollment was unlawful. I should be allowed to graduate retroactively from the 140th OCS on April 14, 1989, and proceed to the Basic School as originally intended. Moreover, I requested an assurance that this type of oversight and neglect would not be allowed to continue. I thought the request was appropriate and the tenor of the letter moderate. But charging racial discrimination was serious business. I showed the letter to Margaret. We both went over it, again and again.

I debated whether to consult Ernie. He had given the Marine Corps twenty years of his life, and might take their side against me. But I decided that, at the very least, I owed him the courtesy of informing him what I was doing. This time I went into the details. He couldn't believe what he was hearing, and was angry that this sort of harassment was still going on. More than twenty years earlier, he too had been subjected to racial remarks when he went through OCS. He became a supporter, and would remain one to the very end. The most important thing he did for me, though, way back in those early days, was believing in me. He never questioned the veracity of my story, never doubted, and never faltered.

120

In January 1990, I was finishing my letter to the commandant. I had a second priority, too: moving out of my parents' house. I had been living at home because I couldn't afford an apartment, but after eight years living on my own in Tokyo and Washington, I needed privacy. I love my mother dearly, but to this day she tends to forget that I am not her teenager anymore. Whenever I left the house, I was subjected to an inquisition:

"So, where are you going?"

"Who are you going out with?"

"You aren't going dressed like that, are you?"

I had to escape, and being unemployed, I had to do it on the cheap. George Sakamoto, my friend from ICU, rescued me. He recently had purchased a condominium and offered me a break on the rent. The unit was small, the carpet and furnishings old. But the lanai offered a panoramic view of the city. It was my little space, close enough, yet far enough from my mother's reach.

My life was on hold. But my hopes were cautiously high. I didn't want to make any professional commitments. A colleague had approached me to work at her law firm. A friend from Japan offered to introduce me to a stream of potential legal clients doing business in Hawaii. I was not interested. The Marine Corps would own up to their mistakes. I naively assumed that in a few months I'd be back in the Corps.

As an emotional escape, I spent time with Baron. I had been away from Hawaii for nine years. Many of my friends were busy with their careers and married with children. I had to accept the fact that the days of getting together to drink beer or shoot hoops on the spur of the moment were long past. Fortunately, Baron was still single. Like me, some of his decisions had not quite panned out as he had hoped. Misery loves company.

"Sure, I'm relatively not busy," he would answer whenever I asked him if we could get together.

With him, I felt free enough to open up, a respite that became more valued as my case against the Corps dragged on. He was passionately supportive of the case, and I could always count on him for a word of inspiration. Several times a week, we would eat lunch in Chinatown or drink coffee at Mocha Java at the Ward Center. We would read the newspaper and spend the afternoon poking fun at each other. The self-deprecating humor would make our sorry lives at least bearable. It must have been the power of laughter, for I always felt rejuvenated.

At one of those lunches with Baron, I first read about Tailhook. On the mainland there was a growing scandal in the military. Navy and Marine Corps aviators allegedly assaulted female officers at a convention in Las Vegas. At the time, it was merely a story that lent credence to my allegations of misconduct at OCS. What I didn't know was that it would serve to focus the nation's attention on problems of discrimination and harassment in the military.

On January 12, 1990, nine months after my disenrollment, I finally sent the letter to the commandant. A few weeks later I received a response.

Dear Mr. Yamashita:

. . . The Commandant has directed me to investigate the matters you raised concerning racial discrimination at the Officer Candidate School, Quantico, VA. Let me assure you, in the strongest possible terms that the Marine Corps neither condones nor tolerates racial remarks or incidents such as those reported in your letter. . . .

Sincerely,
Major General O.K. Steel
Inspector General of the Marine Corps
January 23, 1990

Captain Garcia had been wrong about Marine policy. I could already see myself back in the Corps. Lieutenant Colonel Eugene Brindle was assigned to investigate the case. He spoke with OCS staff and former candidates. He even made a trip to Honolulu.

Colonel Brindle called me from the Hilton Hawaiian Village. I drove down to Waikiki in my dilapidated 1973 VW Beetle to meet him for lunch. We had a corner table at the Rainbow Lanai, fronting Waikiki beach. He greeted me with a firm handshake and a friendly smile. He told me about his experiences in Vietnam. He told me about his travels to exotic places. He told me about various weapon systems. He even explained military tactics used in the Civil War. I patiently waited. At the end of our lunch he finally asked me a few questions about my experience.

"You should take pride that you finished OCS," he concluded.

The lunch ended. We shook hands. I was upbeat. I naively thought that his friendly demeanor could only mean that his report would be favorable.

Once again the initial receptiveness only led to inaction. General Gray stated that the investigation did not find any evidence of discrimination. The Marine Corps brass wanted a whitewash, and Brindle gave it to them. His report was only three pages, poorly organized and filled with grammatical and typographical errors. It acknowledged that Runyun spoke to me in Japanese, but dismissed it as merely an attempt to "put Yamashita at ease." It acknowledged that Carrasco called me by the names of Japanese products, but explained that it was because he had a "general reputation for dyslexic pronunciation of names." It finally concluded there could not have been discrimination, because some of the sergeants involved were African American and Latino. The report absolved the officer corps of responsibility, and implied that it was acceptable for minorities to use racial slurs toward each other. In a seven-page rebuttal I characterized Brindle's report as incredible, said that it was clear that the Marine Corps was unable or unwilling to get its house in order,

123

and vowed to request action from individuals and institutions outside the Corps.

I could feel myself being pulled down a slippery slope. With each passing month the emotional commitment was ratcheted up. I contacted a lawyer, Daphne Barbee. She was eager to meet with me. I showed her my letter to the Marine Corps. Shaking her head in disbelief, she made a few phone calls from her office. I sat at the edge of my chair, trying not to eavesdrop as she asked about cases involving military personnel. I could see the disappointment slowly spreading over her face. She hung up the phone and explained that since I had been in the military, redress would be difficult, if not impossible. Civilian courts defer to the military when it involves personnel decisions. We could proceed, but she could offer little hope.

As I sat there, I couldn't help but recall my meeting with Staff Sergeant Brice during the third week of OCS. He had boasted in the duty hut that he could make "anybody look bad." Those words kept swirling in my head. Now two years later, the Marine Corps was in essence saying it again. They were wrong, but there wasn't a damn thing that I could do about it. They had all the power, and I had none.

The fight was over. Justice would not be done. But as a consolation, Margaret suggested that I do what I had thought about doing at the very beginning: write letters to the Hawaii congressional delegation and civil rights organizations. Maybe they could help. "And even if they can't, if enough of these kinds of letters are sent, someday, somebody will take notice, and there will be change for the better," she said hopefully.

And in that spirit I sent a final round of letters. A few organizations wrote back, but could only offer moral support. The Hawaii congressional delegation—Representative Pat Saiki, Senator Spark Matsunaga, and Senator Inouye—informed me that they had made inquiries. But even Senator Inouye seemed to imply that it was time to move on. He shared a letter that his office had received:

Dear Senator Inouye,

... Mr. Yamashita is looking for reasons outside of himself to fault; regrettably, he does not have the requisite leadership skills to be a Marine officer and should not be commissioned.

Sincerely,
A. M. Gray
General, U.S. Marine Corps
Commandant of the Marine Corps
April 30, 1990

It had been a roller coaster ride. It had been a fool's mission. It was time to move on.

Decision to Fight

SPRING 1990

Dear Mr. Yamashita,

I received your letter of April 17, 1990 regarding your
unfortunate experience at USMC Officer Candidate School
and have forwarded it to our legal counsel for recommended action. As an organization dedicated to the preser-
vation of civil and human rights, we will make every
attempt to fight for justice and equal treatment for all
human beings. Please call me to discuss this matter further.

Sincerely,
William M. Kaneko
President JACL-Honolulu Chapter
May 3, 1990

The Japanese American Citizens League (JACL) is the
oldest Asian American civil rights organization in the
United States. It was founded in 1929 with its headquarters
in San Francisco. It has more than 100 chapters across the
country, including Hawaii. It organizes cultural events,
conducts educational forums, and supports various civil
rights causes. In law school through my involvement in
APALSA, I had attended a few of their functions. But as a
third-generation Japanese American, born and raised in
Hawaii, it held, at the time, little relevance for me. Now it
seemed, JACL might be the most relevant thing in my life.

But I was filled with ambivalence. I had been trying to move on. But once again, I was being pulled back into a fight that I had given up on. I could not help but notice the word "justice" in Mr. Kaneko's letter. I had already learned how difficult achieving it could be. After a week of more sleepless nights, I called Mr. Kaneko. He was articulate, and spoke with the self-assurance of someone with a great deal of real-life experience. A meeting was set up with him and a JACL lawyer, Clayton Ikei, to determine whether they could help me. I arrived early and caught the elevator to the tenth floor of the First Insurance Building on Ward Avenue. The receptionist showed me to a small, modern conference room lined with Hawaii case law, statutes, and legal encyclopedias. She told me that Mr. Ikei was still in court, but that Mr. Kaneko would be with me shortly. A few minutes later there was a polite knock on the door before it swung open. I wonder if my expression mirrored my disappointment. There before me stood a skinny young man with glasses who could have passed for a high school student.

"Hi, I'm Bill Kaneko. Thanks for coming."

Bill had grown up in Hawaii, but had gone to college at the University of the Puget Sound. It was there that he had become involved in civil rights. He was dedicated and spoke with passion, but he was young, in fact, younger than me. My newly discovered enthusiasm started to wane. Was this going to be a keystone cops operation? The blind leading the blind?

When Mr. Ikei arrived, I was relieved that he looked older and a bit more seasoned. He was in a dark business suit, and wore eyeglasses that were accented by his jet black hair neatly combed to one side. I noticed that he walked with a limp. He had been born in Hawaii, but raised in California. He had worked for the Asian Law Caucus in San Francisco, and later the Hawaii Legal Aid Society, providing legal assistance to the indigent. He now had a busy private practice, but squeezed in time to do *pro bono* work for the JACL. We spoke for an hour. Acceptance of the case would mean the commitment of JACL manpower, funds, and prestige.

They invited me to meet with the chapter's board of directors. The board would have to vote; without its approval, there could be no support. The monthly meeting was held at the Richards Street YWCA in downtown Honolulu. I should have asked for advice on how to approach the board, but it was too late. I made a somewhat rambling pitch for support, trying to explain what had happened to me, but finally gave up and stopped. Bill asked for questions. There was an uncomfortable silence. I looked around, trying to read the expressions on noncommitted faces, thinking I had blown my last, best chance. Finally, an elderly woman slowly raised her hand. I held my breath.

"Why would you want to join the Marine Corps in the first place?"

It caught me by surprise. I reacted, almost without thinking. "You're beginning to sound like my mother," I said, smiling.

Everyone laughed and hands began shooting up with question after question about OCS and its implications. There were reservations about getting the chapter involved. Some had lived in Hawaii all of their lives, had never experienced discrimination, and had little interest in it. Others spoke of the Marine Corps' unlimited power and influence. They saw it as a lost cause from the get go.

After I left the meeting, Bill reminded the board of JACL's civil rights mission. He told them that they could do much more than just organize cultural events. If Asian Americans wanted a seat at America's table, then they could no longer play it safe, reaping the benefits secured by the victories of other minority groups. He was particularly troubled that the racial remarks were only directed toward an Asian American. He felt that it would continue until Asians dispelled the view that they were unable or unwilling to organize and fight back.

128

A week went by with no decision. A small part of me was secretly hoping that they wouldn't take the case. I'd be able to claim that I had given it my best shot, and move on with honor. I don't know how he did it. And I didn't ask. But two weeks later Bill contacted me: the JACL-Honolulu chapter would take on the Corps.

We set up a strategy meeting. I invited Ernie to join us. Bill recruited Steve Okino, a feisty former producer for CBS News and a member of the JACL board. He was in his mid-30s, trim and fit, and seemed to think best with a cigarette in his hand. He had been born in Dayton, Ohio, and went to school there and in Chicago. He later worked as a journalist in Chicago, San Francisco, Los Angeles, and Dallas. He was now working for a large public relations firm in Honolulu. He would provide invaluable expertise in getting the media to work for us. Bill, Clayton, Ernie, Steve, and I formed the "inner circle," the individuals who would spearhead the fight.

Legally, my choices were few. Title VII of the Civil Rights Act of 1964 didn't apply to uniformed military personnel. Clayton felt that my best hope was to seek relief from the existing Naval administrative system. If it could not provide relief, then we would sue in federal court. I would be petitioning the Board for Correction of Naval Records (BCNR) to change my unsatisfactory leadership grade to passing. At the same time, I would be petitioning the Naval Discharge Review Board (NDRB) to delete from my record any reference to unsatisfactory leadership.

The Marine Corps would have to take three important steps for there to be a resolution. First, there had to be an acknowledgment of discrimination. Second, there had to be an apology. Third, there had to be a remedy that provided not only redress for me personally, but systemic changes to ensure that it didn't happen again. The problem, we would discover, was that these steps would be difficult to define and the process halting and painfully protracted.

I was reminded of my experiences organizing people to accomplish a task. But this time the playing field was larger, the stakes higher. As the meeting continued, I sat back and listened. My time to lead would come. For in the end, it was my commission that we would be fighting for. I would rely on the expertise of the inner circle. However, I knew there would come a time, when I, and I alone, would have to make the final decision.

We were apprehensive of the reaction from older and younger Japanese Americans. We discussed whether anyone in multiethnic Hawaii would care about a racial discrimination case that occurred 5,000 miles away in Quantico, Virginia. Finally, we wondered whether the fact that some of the OCS staff involved were African American and Latino would make it difficult to build traditional coalitions with other communities of color.

We would have to initiate a legal, political, and media campaign. An important element of the strategy was to educate the public about the case and its broader meaning. This meant appearing on TV and on radio. It meant giving interviews to newspapers. It meant fundraisers and other public appearances. Bill and Steve made it clear: if I wanted to win, then I would have to make my case.

The JACL, the first organization to step forward, was committed. Even at this early stage, there were also individuals who had learned of the case and written letters of support. Moo T. Soo Hoo, a Chinese American who had spent thirty years in the Navy, retiring at the rank of lieutenant commander, wrote to Secretary of the Navy Lawrence Garrett requesting that justice be done. He wrote that in his years in the Navy he was "continuously subjected to racist comments that a Chinese American could not lead Caucasian sailors." Michael F. Yamamoto, a California attorney and Vietnam veteran, wrote to Commandant Gray requesting that this case be reevaluated. Peter Edelman, my constitutional law professor at Georgetown, wrote to several members of Congress requesting their support. Professor Edelman wrote, "I want you to know that you can regard the allegation as credible . . . Bruce is not a person who cries racism lightly."

In these first few tentative months, I was humbled by people like these who courageously spoke out on my behalf. In the ensuing months and years there would be hundreds, if not thousands, who would follow their lead. I was inspired by their commitment and honor-bound to be worthy of their trust.

We were poised for battle, but I began to have doubts. Even with the JACL support I knew that it was a long shot. Most important, my parents wanted me to leave well enough alone: in a fight with the Marine Corps, the only one bloodied and tarnished would be me. I met with Ernie in his office. He had on an aloha shirt that seemed too small for his muscular arms and shoulders. The walls were accented with a few mementos of the Marine Corps. He pointed out a rocket fragment that had almost killed him during the Vietnam War. Ernie had become more than my lawyer. He had become a friend and confidant. He always returned my calls. He always had time to talk. Ernie and I spent the afternoon together. I don't know what I would have done without his simple assurance, "You're doing the right thing . . . it's gonna work out."

Bill had already begun to garner support within the community. Our job was made easier by the fact that Japanese immigrants, like so many other groups, had not arrived in America, dispersed, and immediately acculturated and disappeared into mainstream society. They had established communities wherever they settled. Time and time again we would tap into the network: community organizations, churches, Judo and Ikebana clubs, merchant and veteran groups.

The first groups we contacted were the 442nd Regimental Combat Team and the 100th Battalion. Both were well known and influential in the community. Strategically, their support would be crucial. But would they be willing to stand against the military? Both groups, faced with discrimination, had chosen to fight for their country. I, in contrast, would be challenging it. They might fail to see their connection with my case, brand me unpatriotic, and toss me out the door.

Bill put me in touch with Katsugo Miho, a 442nd RCT veteran and retired state district court judge. In addition to the fact that I was fighting the military, some of the local veterans viewed the JACL, a mainland organization, with distrust. To my surprise and relief, he was supportive. At this early stage, not knowing how people would react, particularly those from the nisei generation, his words of encouragement meant a lot. He arranged a meeting with the 442nd executive board so that I could seek a formal endorsement.

Unlike my meeting with the Honolulu JACL, I prepared for this one. On a sultry afternoon, I arrived at the building on Wiliwili Street they called their "clubhouse." I walked in the door and saw several old men sitting around tables languidly playing cards. They ignored me. I escaped to a far corner of the room, feeling out of place. Fortunately, Judge Miho arrived to save me. He introduced me to twenty veterans who made up their executive committee. I still remember him saying, "By the way, this is Danny Yamashita's nephew." As I spoke, I saw the expressions on their faces change from polite curiosity to interest to concern, then to anger and despair. My voice cracked with emotion as I made my plea. I saw stoic old men unashamedly wiping away tears. One shook his head and said, "We went through all of that fifty years ago for this?!"

Right then, the meaning of my case became clear, and any doubts about my decision to fight vanished. I had heard about the 442nd Regimental Combat Team. Their sacrifices had been payment in full to ensure that my generation's loyalty would never be questioned, and that we could go as far as our talent would take us. But for so many years the significance of that sacrifice had been abstract; now it was staring me in the face. At that moment it was no longer about a single commission and self-interest. It wasn't that laws had been broken or even that there had been an injustice. I realized that at its core our fight was nothing less than vindication for the sweat, indignities and blood of generations past.

133

18

"My Neck Was on the Line"

SUMMER/FALL 1990

IN ORDER TO FIGHT, WE NEEDED PROOF. ERNIE advised me to act quickly before witnesses disappeared. I contacted Gabriel Vargas and Ronnie Catipon. I anxiously waited for two weeks. Of the two I felt closer to Vargas. Our racks had been next to each other. After OCS, he needed time to get his bearings, so I had invited him to stay at the Boston House for a few days. Still on OCS schedule we would wake up early and work out. It was as if, like two little boys in denial, we pretended that we were still in the Marine Corps. For those first few days back in the civilian world, it was good to have someone around. But that was a long time ago.

> I am an American of Bolivian ancestry. I distinctly remember these incidents because I would be offended if I were placed in the same situation as Candidate Yamashita, and subjected to blatantly negative remarks about Bolivia or were spoken to in Spanish. These incidents unfairly singled out Candidate Yamashita implying deficient performance or worse that he was somehow less of an American . . .
>
> Sincerely,
> Gabriel Vargas
> Officer Candidate, 140th OCS
> July 31, 1990

Catipon's letter followed shortly thereafter. He had been asked to verify the "Ultra-man" incident that had occurred in the squad bay.

> . . . It served no useful purpose other than to humiliate him in front of his peers, denigrate his status as a candidate, and to single him out as an individual minority in a situation where conformity to the group is of paramount importance. I believe that this incident, along with other incidents previously documented, only served to single out and highlight Candidate Yamashita from the rest of the candidates in the platoon, and in doing this, subject him to more harmful ridicule, scorn, and scrutiny from the staff and his peers at OCS.
>
> Sincerely,
> Ronnie S. Catipon
> Officer Candidate, 140th OCS
> August 7, 1990

But both Vargas and Catipon had been disenrolled. I needed verifications from active duty Marines. I carefully made a list of candidates who had graduated, and with whom I felt comfortable approaching: Woolfolk, Wagner, Cederholm, Pugh. I knew many were on aviation contracts.

I called Pensacola Naval Air Station's main switchboard. The only person they could locate was Cederholm. I was apprehensive about making the call. For nine weeks we had been comrades; now we were worlds apart. Now he was an officer of Marines; I was a reject. He answered the phone cordially. But as we talked his demeanor changed. I asked him about the incidents, but he said he remembered nothing about them. It was clear that Cederholm knew how to protect his career. It was equally clear that getting help from my former colleagues, who were now officers of Marines, would be far more difficult than I had imagined.

Without verifications from active duty Marines, I had no case. But I had come too far to quit. I called the Marine

Corps World Wide Locator, a listing of all active duty Marines. The sergeant who answered the phone was impatient, and said he could not locate any of the other names. It was another dead end. I dreaded calling Clayton to pull the plug on the case. A week went by; I was obsessed that **136** they were out there somewhere. With no options left, I called the World Wide Locator again. The corporal on duty could not locate the names, but he peppered me with questions about the candidates: Age? Ground contract? Aviation contract? Social security number? He found Wagner and Woolfolk. It pays, I was reminded, to be persistent. And what a crap shoot it was, all dependent upon who happens to pick up the phone. I will forever be indebted to that unknown corporal who took the time to go the extra mile for a stranger. He will never know that, but for him, the case would have been lost.

Wagner was in Jackson, Mississippi. His wife answered. We played phone tag for a week. Trying not to sound desperate, I told him how important his verification was to my case. I recalled the last time I saw Wagner. I had been disenrolled and returned to Charlie Company. Pitts had ordered candidates to help me. My wall locker had flown open, and my foot locker had been dragged to the middle of the squad bay. The contents had been poured into a duffel bag. All of us had been through hell together, and whether we liked it or not a bond had been formed. Wagner had come across the squad bay to say good-bye. A man of few words, I could see on his face what he was feeling. He was as bewildered as I, as to what was happening.

Two weeks later I received a letter. In his final paragraph Wagner wrote:

> I believe that Candidate Yamashita was subjected to tougher scrutiny than any other candidate at OCS. It seemed that the OCS staff was doing everything in their power to ensure that Candidate Yamashita would not graduate. This was unfair in light of the fact that the OCS staff

appeared to bend over backwards to assist other candidates who were struggling in PT, or spent weeks in sick bay.

Sincerely,
Second Lt. Michael Wagner
United States Marine Corps
September 27, 1990   **137**

I contacted Woolfolk, but was particularly concerned about his reaction. After all, many of the incidents involved Marines who were also African American. Throughout the case as I spoke to individuals and groups, this African-on-Asian discrimination at the 140th OCS had the potential of reducing our struggle for justice into an intra-minority turf war. But for Woolfolk, it was a nonissue. Without hesitation, he sent a letter verifying the incidents.

In the case of a simple uncontested petition for a change in discharge status or correction of a record, filling out a simple one-page form provided by the respective boards would have sufficed. However, my case would require an affidavit that would lay out the background of the case, cite specific violations of the regulations, and present arguments why these violations tainted the evaluation. I pored over hundreds of pages of documents written, not in plain English, but in a prose invented by bureaucrats. The more I read, the more obsessed I became in trying to first decipher the language, then in finding a paragraph, a sentence, even a phrase that had some bearing on my case.

Although it was the last thing in the world I wanted to do, I knew that my research would not be complete without a trip back to Quantico. I needed to look over my OCS records and any other documents available. I flew into Washington, D.C., and took the Amtrak to Quantico. It was so different from the winter I had spent there: hot and humid, the trees covered with thick green foliage.

As I peered out the train window, I reflected on how mere chance affects our lives. I couldn't help but think how things could have been different had I not been transferred to Brice's platoon. Or perhaps if I had marched into Colonel Reinke's office after the first incident in protest. What if I had accepted the offer from the Army JAG? Or just joined a law firm? Still peering out the window, I was overcome **138** with regret.

I caught a taxi from the town of Quantico to the battalion headquarters, where I had been officially disenrolled by Colonel Reinke. The 140th OCS staff had been transferred to new assignments. But a part of me could still feel the overbearing presence of Brice. In my civilian clothes, on my mission to gather evidence against the Corps, I felt like a spy infiltrating the enemy. A Marine showed me to a room where my OCS records were lying on the table.

"You can make copies down the hall," he said over his shoulder as he left the room.

I grabbed a stack of documents. I passed the barbershop, and happened to peer into one of the rooms. Sitting there behind a desk was an officer with short-cropped blond hair reading the newspaper: Lieutenant Eshelman! All the memories came rushing back. Now that we were on a level playing field, a part of me wanted to burst into the room and confront him. But I reminded myself of the purpose of my return to OCS, and instead, slipped away without a word.

Another crucial aspect of the struggle would be the support of Senator Inouye. I had already been in touch with the other members of the Hawaii congressional delegation. But as chairman of the Senate Defense Appropriations Sub-Committee, he had the power and clout. Fortunately, I thought I might have a connection.

So after finishing in Quantico, I met with Jennifer Goto, a classmate from Georgetown who had risen to be one of Inouye's top advisers. She was as I had remembered her. She looked young for her age, and she still had those big eyes and round cheeks. We had both been in APALSA, where she had been assigned to be my "big sister," or student mentor.

It had been a good relationship; we often poked fun at each other. But that was a long time ago. I had no idea what her reaction might be. Knowing about the APALSA party fisaco, she could argue that this is another fine mess that I should clean up myself. Indeed, it was easy to imagine her playfully accusing me of just joining the Corps to increase my sex appeal with the "chicks."

When I entered Inouye's office the atmosphere was officious. I slowly climbed up some steps to her office, which was smaller than I expected. We joked with each other and reminisced. The office had made routine inquiries to the Marine Corps on my behalf, but this was the first time that Jennifer had heard the details. She became serious, and then indignant. She made me promise to keep her in the loop.

Buoyed by my trip to the East Coast, I returned to Honolulu. I began dating Carol Kawamura. She was attractive, bright, and independent. She lived in Kahalu'u on the other side of the island, which gave me an excuse to drive out to the country. The fresh air and magnificent view of the rugged slopes of the Ko'olau mountains were rejuvenating. On the weekends, we would go out for dinner and then hang out at my place and watch videos. Carol, while no civil rights activist, was supportive of my efforts, but more important provided a perspective on life outside the case

I began drafting the legal affidavit that would be submitted to the Naval Boards. August came and went. Clayton had been calling me for progress reports. He wanted to submit everything as soon as possible. But, after several rewrites, both Margaret and I were not satisfied with it. In September, as I walked into his office, the tension in the air was like a slap in the face.

"Is it ready?"

I steeled myself.

"I need more time," I said firmly.

Clayton's face tightened. "Well, if you don't want to do this, just tell me. Don't waste my damn time!"

I stared at Clayton. And he stared back. I didn't want to say anything that I would regret, and neither did he. I assured him that the affidavits would be ready in a few weeks. I would find Clayton moody and difficult to get along with. But what got me through the aggravating moments was realizing that he was the only game in town, and the one that would stand with me to the end.

140

By late September everything was ready. Margaret had spent hours, if not days, editing. I was proud of the finished product. It had taken time, but I believed it was time well spent. The completed petitions and affidavits would be carefully scrutinized not only by the respective boards, but by journalists, lawyers, leaders of organizations, and public officials.

The filing of the petitions and the affidavits would be the first shot across the bow. It would officially initiate our case against the Marine Corps. With the JACL involved, Margaret gracefully, or perhaps gladly, began to relinquish her hands-on role in the case, and instead, became my loudest cheerleader. I will never forget that she was there in the beginning when I needed her most.

My parents continued to have doubts. Their lives had been spent working within the system, not fighting it. There's a Japanese expression: the nail that sticks out will be hammered back into its place. But I couldn't just casually move on with my life. I felt like my back was up against a cliff with a raging river in front of me. To "move on" I had to dive in and swim. Margaret finally convinced them that I was doing the right thing. "You didn't send him to law school just to draft lease agreements, did you?" she lectured. My parents still doubted, but as they had done all my life, in the end, they threw me their support.

Before the official announcement, I needed to sign the petitions and affidavits. Only Clayton, the notary public, and I were present. "Are you sure you wanna do this?"

From left to right, Clayton, I, and Bill at our first press conference, 1990. Photo courtesy of *The Hawaii Herald*.

Clayton said in a low voice. I looked up at him. I was a bit surprised at the question.

"Because the bottom line is that even with all your supporters, in the end, it's your neck on the line," he continued.

We had notified the news media about our filing. Steve was pacing Clayton's office, wondering whether the press would show. The Sunday before, he had organized a mock interview with cameras and lights. He had written out a summary statement. He had warned me of hostile questions, but instructed me to return to our basic message. We had gone over it again and again. He had even told me what to wear. Right on schedule the various reporters checked in: Stu Glauberman of the *Honolulu Advertiser*, Ben Seto of the *Honolulu Star-Bulletin*, Kelli Abe of KGMB, Paul Udell of KITV, and Ray Lovell of KHON. The lights flashed on, the camera rolled, and with Clayton and Bill at my side, we did one interview after another.

"You'll be on the news at 6. I'll call you," said Steve.

That evening I sat alone in my bedroom, and cringed as

I watched the story lead the local news. There was no turning back.

"JAPANESE AMERICAN ACCUSES MARINES OF BIAS"
(*Honolulu Star-Bulletin* 10-19-90)

"AJA OCS CANDIDATE CHARGES DISCRIMINATION"
(*Honolulu Advertiser* 10-19-90)

"BRUCE YAMASHITA: RACISM IN THE MARINE CORPS?"
(*Hawaii Herald* 11-2-90)

There were Letters to the Editor attacking me. There was criticism on talk radio. There was a rambling letter with a drawing of me in effigy, stating that "he SHOULD go back to his own country!" Clayton received a letter that threatened, "there will be a death warrant on Bruce, if you proceed." One letter reminded me of the sneak attack on Pearl Harbor.

But these responses galvanized support from individuals who otherwise would have remained silent. They responded with their own Letters to the Editor, and calls to radio talk shows. It forced the multicultural and multi-ethnic community to confront the issue of racism. A line in the sand was slowly being drawn. Clayton was right. My neck was on the line.

19

Face-Off

SPRING 1991

I₁ was time to confront the Marine Corps, face to face. We drove up Halawa Heights, which provided a panoramic view of Pearl Harbor. The sky was blue. The sun was shining. As I looked in the back seat, I saw Ernie. I remembered the last time I had driven up this road in 1988. I could still see him, "Major Kimoto," standing in the parking lot in his green cammies. He had told me that the Corps needed people like me, particularly in Japan and the Far East. I had been sold on the idea that, unlike other branches of the military, the Marine Corps required all officers, including lawyers, to complete Officer Candidate School. His parting words again echoed in my ears:

"Lawyers in the other branches go through a two-week charm course, but in the Marine Corps you earn your bars. In the Marine Corps you are an officer first, and a lawyer second."

I felt a burst of excitement. But a bump in the road snapped me back to reality. As we continued our drive up the heights, I reflected on the frenzied activity of the past few months which had brought me back to the U.S. Pacific Command, Camp H. M. Smith.

Dear Mr. Ikei,

> . . . Upon review of Mr. Yamashita's petition, it was apparent that he has raised new allegations . . . Although the preliminary inquiry . . . did not substantiate Mr. Yamashita's allegations of racial discrimination, the Commandant of the Marine Corps has directed an Inspector General Investigation . . .

Sincerely,
J. R. Williams Colonel, USMC
Deputy Inspector General
November 9, 1990

144

It had been an important first step, and a lesson in the power of public opinion. Steve had continued to make the media work for us.

"MARINES WILL RE-OPEN DISCRIMINATION CASE"
(*Honolulu Advertiser* 11-27-90)

"DISCRIMINATION CASE BY MANOA MAN AGAINST MARINES REOPENED" (*Honolulu Star-Bulletin* 11-27-90)

Bill had wanted not just a new investigation, but a fair one, and had urged those in the community to continue the pressure. Senator Inouye and other members of the Hawaii congressional delegation had sent letters to government officials. The National Asian Pacific American Bar Association and Hawaii Women Lawyers had endorsed the case. Other individuals and groups from the mainland had written simple, but powerful letters of support. Dr. David Takeuchi of the UCLA National Research Center on Asian American Mental Health had written a letter to the Navy attacking the logic and findings of the first Marine investigation.

That summer Saddam Hussein had invaded Kuwait and UN forces took up position in the Persian Gulf. The airwaves had been filled with images of proud Marines, sailors, soldiers, and airmen being deployed to the region. As the case was as much a public relations battle as a legal one, the inner circle agreed that we should temporarily keep a low profile and support our troops. In early 1991, Operation Desert Storm had liberated Kuwait, and with the troops out of harm's way we had resumed our attacks.

I had stormed into Bill's office livid. Although I had promised to keep Woolfolk's and Wagner's identities under **145** wrap, I had learned that their names had appeared in the press. They made it clear that they had felt betrayed, and that I should no longer contact them. I knew from the beginning as active duty marines how difficult it had been for them to come forward. They had nothing to gain other than the satisfaction of doing what was right. Not only had we lost valuable allies; but I had lost two friends. Bill did not know how it could have happened. As I stood in his office I had wanted answers. Bill placed his eyeglasses on his desk, and rubbed his eyes as if to wipe away frustration.

"Listen, I'm sorry . . . It's a setback, a bump in the road. But we gotta deal with it and move on," Bill had said in a firm voice with a finger pointing at me.

It had been the first time that I saw Bill flash such emotion. I realized that he was right. Bill had not only been the first to recognize the significance of the case, he was critical to managing its execution. My initial fears that it would be the "blind leading the blind" had been unfounded. He was a great communicator with boundless energy and optimism. Whenever there was a problem, he was the one that had ten different ideas on how to solve it.

Bill had sought the endorsement of the Hawaii State Legislature, which was another reminder of how important it was that I was from Hawaii. I began to appreciate why Catipon and Vargas, both raised on the mainland, had refused to take on the case themselves. Representatives Carol Fukunaga and Tom Okamura, fellow delegates at the Constitutional Convention, had agreed to be the co-sponsors of the resolution in the state House. We would present testimony before the House Inter-Governmental

Relations Committee. As luck would have it, Les Ihara and Clarice Hashimoto, chair and vice-chair respectively, were familiar faces, for they too had been delegates to the convention. Members of the public submitted testimony both in favor of and against the resolution. But the most moving testimony had been that of Eric Yamamoto, law professor at the University of Hawaii Law School and my freshmen basketball coach at University Lab School. He had spoken eloquently on the issue of civil rights, and with his substantial credibility offered powerful support for the resolution. But, I must say, with all the negative Letters to the Editor, and other disparaging comments I was hearing, my self-esteem had taken a beating. What I remember most was what he said about me as a person.

146

> *Bruce had the respect of every teammate and, perhaps equally important, the aloha of his teammates' families who often came to the games. He was special then. A leader. And it is particularly ironic that the Marine trainers last year cited "lack of leadership" as the pretext for dismissing Bruce just before graduation. So many groups, so many people have rallied behind Bruce. His mother recently told me that her initial fears and hesitation have been transformed into proud support. Bruce has suffered an injustice. He is speaking out and demanding acknowledgment and redress. He is speaking out not only for himself but for us all.*

"Remember, how you say it and how you appear is just as important as what you say," implored Clayton, interrupting my reverie and snapping me back to the moment.

We came to the main gate of Camp Smith. Ernie flashed his ID indicating that he was a retired officer. The corporal gave a crisp salute and waved us through. This was Ernie's old stomping grounds. His expertise and experience proved to be invaluable. Throughout the case, he was the one that understood military law and could interpret Marine Corps correspondence. He was the one that had served with individuals that we were dealing with, and could provide insights into what was happening behind the scenes at Marine Corps headquarters.

As we walked across the yard toward the building, I tried to make small talk with Ernie, hoping that it would loosen the knots in my stomach. I also couldn't help but notice Clayton's limp and the physical energy that he had to exert in order to keep up with us. It seemed an appropriate metaphor for the inner circle's collective determination and grit.

Colonel James Williams, a tall Marine officer, met us at the door. I stepped ahead and shook his hand firmly. We were shown to a room with a conference table. Across from us were Williams, deputy inspector general; Lieutenant Colonel Les Roth, head of the Assistance, Investigations, and Administration Branch; and Captain Gregory Mitchell, judge advocate general. I suspected that it wasn't a coincidence that the Corps had sent Mitchell, a black officer.

The hearing convened at 1337 hours. Williams gave a brief introduction. I thanked them for coming to speak with us in person. But remembering my hours of small talk with Lieutenant Colonel Brindle, I wanted to get down to business. I asked point blank whether racial remarks were allowed at OCS. Colonel Williams appeared uncomfortable with the question.

"The Marine Corps' regulations prohibit using racial slurs. But it's very simple to say 'absolutely not' . . . each instance you have to determine what did take place."

"What about Kawasaki Yamaha Yamashita?" I asked, leaning toward him.

"I think at this point I am not going to be interviewed, okay?"

I gave him a confused look. He tried to explain what he meant.

"For example, if there are two candidates with the name 'Kelley' in the platoon, the sergeants for convenience might give one of them a nickname."

"But there was only one 'Yamashita,'" I deadpanned across the table.

Captain Mitchell, intent on changing the subject and beginning his interview, interrupted us. He went over the various incidents to determine whether they were made out of malice toward race. I asserted that they were. He then pursued other lines of questioning. Who were my buddies at OCS? Was there any positive feedback at the review boards? Did I complain of the unfair treatment? The questions continued into the afternoon.

"Tell you what, . . . according to the clock it's a little after 1520. Why don't we take a break and defer to my bladder?" said Colonel Williams.

I went to the head and stood in front of the urinal. A few moments passed when Captain Mitchell came up beside me in front of the next urinal. There was an awkward silence.

"It angers me that this sort of stuff is still going on down there," he said to me in a low voice.

For a moment I felt a bond with him. But my experience with Brice was too fresh in my mind. Was this just another ploy to throw me off guard and set me up for failure? Was Mitchell, like Brice, just a pawn in the system? Could he be resentful of a discrimination complaint by an Asian against blacks? But wanting to take advantage of the overture, I asked him what else he knew about the investigation. Suddenly, Colonel Williams burst into the head, ending our conversation before it could begin.

The meeting reconvened. The questions continued to determine whether the remarks toward me were racially motivated. The interview then turned to the performance of other candidates. I told them about Candidate Kempster, who was on light duty for weeks. I told them about Webster, who failed the endurance run. They assured me that they would pull their files and do some comparisons. We took another short break. Colonel Williams then informed us that his target date for completion was April. The meeting

148

was coming to a close. Then he asked a series of questions that I didn't expect.

"So what do you want?"

"I want to be a Marine."

"Do you want a particular Military Occupational Specialty?"

"Judge advocate."

"Do you want your commission effective April 14, 1989?"

"Yes, Sir."

Four hours after we had begun, the colonel went off the record. As we drove down Halawa Heights, I savored the colorful sunset and a feeling of accomplishment. I was convinced that I would soon be commissioned an officer of Marines. What I didn't know was that this was only an initial skirmish. There would be many battles ahead. The fight had just begun.

20

"Totally Unacceptable"

COLONEL WILLIAMS' APRIL COMPLETION DATE came and went. It would take several more months. Still optimistic, I felt that this delay could only mean good news. As I saw it, if it was to be a simple denial, they would have told us already.

In the meantime I kept busy. I began to help my brother-in-law with his law practice, and began assisting two Japanese companies doing business in Hawaii. My work with the companies was fun: viewing construction sites, attending meetings, eating at fancy restaurants, and playing golf. It was a "bubble economy," with banks providing easy credit to their customers. The work helped to pay the bills.

Every Sunday I would return home for a family dinner. Their stable lives only emphasized the uncertainty of mine. My parents worried about my future. Everyone asked me about the case. With all the publicity, whether at work or at play, they had become associated with the case. I tried to paint as positive a picture as possible. I assured them that I'd be hearing from the Marine Corps soon.

The Hawaii State Legislature had passed the concurrent resolution of support. We were now lobbying the Hawaii congressional delegation. I made a trip to Washington in August. Congressman Neil Abercrombie, newly elected

My Japanese clients and I at a golf course on the island of Kauai, 1991.

member of the Hawaii delegation who sat on the House Armed Services Committee, would coordinate the resolution.

At Congressman Abercrombie's office, I gave the receptionist my name. She rang the communications director, Mike Slackman. He was soft spoken, but exuded competence and caring. He showed me to his cubicle. I squeezed into an open chair surrounded by unopened boxes. We had been talking about the wording of the resolution for about twenty minutes, when we heard the congressman's voice in the outer office.

Abercrombie's personal office had mementos and plaques decorating the walls. He stood in the middle of the office. He was not tall, but had a barrel chest. His face had a wide grin on it, which was accented by heavy brown-rimmed glasses and a grayish beard. He wore a dark suit, but I could not keep my eyes off his cowboy boots.

"Thank you for all the support," I said shaking his hand.

"No, thank YOU," he said firmly.

I urged him to support the resolution.

"I'll sign that resolution, and will support you, but only if you are willing to go all the way; I'm not going to do it if you're gonna quit."

152

I nodded. He stood up, came around his desk, and gave me a bear hug. From that meeting on, I always felt welcome at his office. It reinforced my belief that leadership starts at the top. Whenever I called Mike Slackman there was a rare openness: he was always ready to help, give advice, or just shoot the breeze.

Back home in Hawaii, it had been a long, hot summer. Finally, in August 1991, five months after the IG (Inspector General) interview and almost two and a half years since my disenrollment, I received word from the Corps.

Dear Mr. Yamashita,

. . . The investigation revealed that . . . certain instructors, in their . . . application of controlled stress . . . did at various times inappropriately use this tool. This was done by focusing on your ethnic heritage . . . and for this an apology is extended. . . .

Sincerely,
H. E. Davison
Major General, USMC
Deputy Naval Inspector General
Washington D.C.
August 30, 1991

The first IG report had implied that I was a liar. This report substantiated or partially substantiated at least ten of my allegations. It concluded that certain sergeant instructors at the 140th OCS had violated Marine Corps regulations. Although they were careful to use the words "ethnic insensitivity," to me it was a de facto acknowledg-

Congressman Neil Abercrombie and I after our meeting, 1991.

ment that discrimination had occurred. Most important, the Marine Corps had apologized.

But the proposed remedy was totally unacceptable. There would be no commission. All it offered was the "opportunity" to reenter OCS and recompete for a commission. More than two years after I had finished OCS, they expected me to start over! Moreover, it failed to make any policy changes that would ensure that this would not happen again. Finally, the report placed the blame at the feet of the enlisted personnel. It failed to hold the officers of the 140th OCS accountable. Of course, none of the officers who had so bravely mocked me at the final review were now willing to step forward to accept responsibility. I recalled the words of Captain Rodenbeck instilling in us, on that first day of OCS, that an officer was responsible and accountable for anything that happened on his "watch." Had this standard suddenly changed? Or was it all bullshit?

Clayton and I in the rotunda of the Hawaii State Capitol speaking with reporters, 1991. Photo courtesy of *The Hawaii Herald.*

If this was Marine Corps leadership, then once again, it was the sort of leadership that I didn't understand.

I fired back a point-by-point response. I wrote that the report had given lip service to the Equal Opportunity Manual (EOM) and related regulations, taken an arrogant and self-serving attitude toward the investigation, and still refused to pay full penance for the acknowledged transgressions. I reasserted that if the Marine Corps was serious about nondiscrimination then they would commission me retroactively, taking into account the years that had passed since 1989.

Meeting with reporters in the rotunda of the state capitol in Honolulu, I vowed to fight on.

"COMMISSION DEMANDED, DESPITE CORPS APOLOGY"
(*Honolulu Advertiser* 9-14-91)

"MANOA MAN WINS APOLOGY FROM MARINES"
(*Honolulu Star Bulletin* 9-14-91)

"BRUCE YAMASHITA TO FIGHT ON"
(*Hawaii Herald* 9-20-91)

Confident, I waited for a reply. After several anxious months, it slowly dawned on me that there would be no response. The Marine Corps' offer was final.

"Barely above Water"

WINTER 1991–SPRING 1992

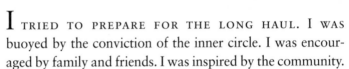

I TRIED TO PREPARE FOR THE LONG HAUL. I WAS buoyed by the conviction of the inner circle. I was encouraged by family and friends. I was inspired by the community.

Melvin Ezer, my mother's colleague in the College of Education and a friend of the family for over thirty years, asked me to speak to his class. A week after my presentation, I received a letter from him.

Dear Bruce:

It was a powerful but poignant story that you related with humor and grace. I believe your testimony made the students face a truth that our society has a sickness which may affect them directly, and yet for which they may hold a cure. Your willingness to describe your own thoughts and feelings; your fears and insecurities; and your resolve and determination to right a wrong, not only for yourself, but for all of us can serve as model and inspiration. You were able to accomplish in a short time what I have been striving for all semester; to have students understand that each of us has the obligation to move our society toward the ideals of "liberty and justice for all."

Aloha,
Melvin Ezer
Professor of Education

I spoke at the 442nd RCT forty-ninth annual banquet before 600 veterans and their families. They had been there with their support every time we called them. After my speech I was surrounded by family and friends. Judge Miho came up to shake my hand. Another veteran introduced me to his two grandchildren. Uncle Daniel reminded me how proud he was. I had no idea where the case was going, but the banquet was a reminder of why we had to push on.

Hawaii's multiethnic and multicultural community continued to inspire me: the big burly truck driver on Ke'eaumoku street who flashed a "shaka" sign and a big smile; the high school student who stopped me at Ala Moana Shopping Center to wish me luck; the retiree who tapped me on the shoulder and donated a crinkled five dollar bill.

"I'm rooting for you," she whispered as she got on the bus.

The 442nd veteran who gave me a book by Peter Irons entitled *The Courage of Their Convictions*. "Take heart no matter what you do the rest of your life nothing could be prouder . . . Take heart!" he said as he gave me a thumbs-up.

But the reality was that I was losing heart. The case had lost momentum. It now would have to work its way through the administrative process, which could take years. The media had rushed off to other stories. It appeared that supporters had begun to lose interest. I had doubts whether it ever would be resolved.

Carol and I broke up. We had continued to see each other over the past year. She had always been there to give a word of support, but still sensitive enough to know that I needed my space. But she was in her early 30s, and had wanted a serious relationship, which I could not give to her. I had become increasingly antisocial, avoiding the public whenever possible. And when Carol did drag me out, I had hounded her to leave early. But I knew that she had been there for me during the worst of it. I will never forget that she stood by me not when I was riding high, but when I was at my lowest.

With the mounting frustration my health began to suffer. I was always tired. After a meal I would have belching fits. I had stiffness across my back. I had difficulty concentrating. I saw several doctors, but they couldn't find anything wrong with me. So I began to exercise, practice Tai Chi, and take long saunas. It didn't help.

Years later I would fully understand the link between mind and body and the power of one's attitude. Throughout the case I kept thinking, Someday I'll be happy. I kept telling myself I'd be okay after the case was resolved. Instead of seeing it as an opportunity for growth, I saw it as a huge burden. What I didn't appreciate was that life was passing me by. Friends were getting married. Nieces and nephews were growing up. Parents were getting old. Looking back, I should have counted my blessings instead of my problems. I should have gone camping and done a little more fishing. I should have realized that the struggle was a marathon, not a 100-yard dash. I should have realized that great things can be accomplished without driving oneself into the ground.

"Bruce, you should be ashamed of yourself. Let's face it, you just didn't have what it took. My sons went to the Air Force Academy and made it. You're a disgrace!" he shouted waving his cigar at me.

As 1991 neared an end, the JACL was gearing up for the fiftieth anniversary of the Japanese attack on Pearl Harbor. They wanted to ensure that the events focused on the lessons of the past, not racial hysteria. As part of the festivities, I participated in a panel discussion. The man with the cigar was George Yoshinaga, a war veteran and columnist for the *Rafu Shimpo*, the largest Japanese American newspaper based on the mainland. He had been critical of the case from the beginning. He thought I was unpatriotic and a hypocrite. And he wasn't alone. There were many

158

others like him both in and outside the community. Some felt that racial remarks were necessary to make tough Marines. Others believed that charging racism had become a convenient excuse for many. Still others spoke about racism against whites and native Hawaiians.

We desperately needed something to jumpstart the case. **159** Then ABC News "20/20" contacted us. With Steve's guidance, I put together a packet and sent it off to New York. We made the first cut. The producer asked whether I had plans to be in New York City. I had none, but was convinced that a face-to-face meeting could make the difference. I told her that I did. Of course, with money tight, I had no choice but to put the cost of airfare on my credit card.

I flew into Washington and took the Amtrak to New York City. From New York Penn Station I took a taxi, and after getting lost, arrived at ABC headquarters. Running late, I briefly looked up to marvel at the massive building before I jumped on a crowded elevator. I waited in the lobby before the producer appeared. She was a young African American woman who was genuinely interested in the story. She introduced me to the executive producer. No decision could be made. Like everything else, it would take time.

Before leaving New York, I called Bill to update him on my meeting and to tell him that I would stop in Los Angeles before returning to Hawaii.

"Are you crazy . . . LA is going up in smoke!"

I had completely missed the news that an all-white jury had acquitted the police officers involved in the beating of Rodney King. Rioters in the black community protested the verdict. Scene after scene of violence was now on CNN. I cringed when I saw Korean merchants protecting their property with guns. Rumors flew that unrest was spreading to other cities across the nation; in New York rioters were preparing to block traffic on the Brooklyn Bridge. Looking from my hotel room across the Manhattan skyline, the view was surreal.

"20/20" decided to drop the story. All that time and money to come to New York had been spent for nothing. I was convinced that the combination of Asian, Marine Corps, and discrimination was not mainstream enough for the East Coast media establishment. I recalled my meeting with Peter Okada and his insight that as an Asian American he was neither "fish nor fowl." I began to understand more and more what he meant.

When I returned to Hawaii, Senator Inouye was beginning his reelection campaign. He hosted a gala fundraiser, which seemed more like a coronation than a kick-off for a political campaign. It was clear that this event was for Hawaii's movers and shakers in the political and business community. At the time, we didn't know that his opponent would produce a secretly taped conversation accusing him of sexual misconduct. Amidst denials, the transcripts would be splashed on the front page of the local newspapers. Overnight the coronation would turn into a nasty campaign. Our immediate concern would be the impact it would have on his ability to push the case forward. Our longer-term fear was the thought that he might actually lose the election. It would give him a scare, but in the end, he was easily reelected to a fifth term. But in the spring of 1992, we knew none of this.

It had been three years since my disenrollment. With the Marine Corps' acknowledgment of racial harassment, we believed that the time was right for a complete resolution. Bill and I waited in a reception line that circled the room, and then extended out the door. We were hoping for a verbal commitment that the senator would make a final push.

"Bruce Yamashita . . . Thanks for all the help, Senator."

There wasn't a word about the case. There wasn't a word of encouragement. There wasn't even a glimmer of recognition. Although we thought the case was the most important story in town, the cold reality was that he had no idea who we were. After all the disappointments over the previous eight months, I was beginning to believe that the case was doomed.

In June I went over to my parents' house for Sunday dinner. Pop had become a staunch supporter. I noticed that he had clipped articles on the case, and had them neatly stacked on his desk. It was during dinner that I noticed a small dark spot on his left cheek. He came from a tough generation.

"Ah, it's nothing . . . I feel fine!" he responded as he impatiently rubbed it with his hand.

But he was diagnosed with angiosarcoma, a rare and aggressive form of cancer. He had surgery to remove the tissue, and immediately began radiation treatment. After months of one setback after another, his cancer could not have come at a worse time.

I was barely above water. The decision to fight the Marine Corps had become a colossal mistake. I wondered whether justice would ever be done. As a child I had gone to Sunday School. But as the years passed, my connection to the church had been reduced to yearly visits to the Christmas candlelight service. Religion had become more tradition than anything else. I had come to believe that out of sheer will I could control my life. But I was beginning to be humbled by the realization that there's God's plan and my plan, and maybe my plan doesn't count. Now more than ever, I found myself returning to my childhood, and stealing a moment to say a quiet prayer.

22

The Tide Begins to Turn

IN 1992 BILL CLINTON BECAME THE FORTY-SECOND president of the United States. I did not know it at the time, but this shift of power and ideology would have a huge impact on the case. One of his first initiatives, despite opposition from the military establishment, was the lifting of the ban on gays serving in the military. Years earlier I would not have recognized the parallels between the gay movement and myself. Now it was crystal clear.

I listened to the arguments of the military establishment. It reminded me of the type of rhetoric used to justify their actions in my case. Some argued that the AIDS virus would infect the military blood supply. They ignored the fact that there are standard procedures to ensure that this would not happen whether the population source is gay or straight. Others warned of rampant physical groping and molestation in the barracks and the field. They forget that this sort of conduct would be unacceptable even among heterosexual personnel, the most visible example being the Tailhook scandal. Some produced the survey results of enlisted personnel that showed that the rank and file were overwhelmingly against the lifting of the ban. But when was the last time the military brass based a major policy decision on what the troops wanted? A policy affecting civil rights should be based not on a poll, on the whims of the majority, but on whether it is right or wrong.

Those in opposition are on the wrong side of history. Most thought the inclusion of blacks would disrupt unit cohesion. Many argued that women could never be integrated into the military. There were voices of protest to an all-volunteer force because it could never be entrusted to protect our national security. Over the years, dedicated men and women, in war and peace, have time and time again proven the doubters wrong.

163

After much opposition, President Clinton abandoned a total lifting of the ban and settled on "don't ask, don't tell." It was not perfect, but it was certainly a major step in the right direction. But from the perspective of my current struggle, I knew that they had a long way to go. Even if the ban was someday fully lifted, this would not prevent a military superior from submitting unfair fitness reports or turning a blind eye to harassment simply because he did not like homosexuals. Fifty years since the interment and after the last soldier of the 442nd RCT returned home from Europe, I knew firsthand the difficulty of changing not just the law of the land, but the attitude of individuals.

In the spring of 1993 I would watch on television a Gay Rights March on Washington. I was especially moved by the crowds of gay men and lesbians in their 50s and 60s. I could only imagine the humiliation and fear they had to endure during a lifetime of silence. They were entrepreneurs, journalists, teachers, engineers, lawyers, and doctors, who day in and day out did their jobs with dignity and made their contribution to America. The march was a message of hope and a celebration of freedom. And a reminder that should our freedom be threatened, we should be able to count on all Americans, gay and straight, to defend it.

But in 1992, I was not fighting for gay rights, but with the NDRB. They had notified us that our appearance in

Washington, D.C., would be scheduled over the summer. We began our preparations. Then more correspondence:

Dear Mr. Yamashita,

... An additional review of your microfiche personnel file indicates there is no reason for a personal appearance hearing before the NDRB. . . . Your case has been closed without further action. . . .

Sincerely,
R. E. Zimmerman
Captain, JAGC, USN
July 17, 1992

Clayton sent a letter of protest. Steve began preparing to hold a press conference. Then the NDRB reversed course, notifying us that the letter had been an "inadvertent mistake." But they argued that they could make a decision based on the documents submitted. We agreed, provided that if we were not satisfied with their decision, then they would allow us to make an appearance before the board in Washington, D.C.

On August 26, the NDRB notified us of its decision: it lacked authority to change the reason for my disenrollment and it could not provide a retroactive commission, back pay, or service credit. The board only had the authority to change the basis of my separation from *"Entry Level Separation"* to *"Entry Level Separation/Determination of Service Secretary-Secretary of the Navy Plenary Authority."* I had no idea what it meant. But Ernie assured me that it was a small step in the right direction. I had jumped through the bureaucratic hoops. I wanted my day in court.

By now there was an important addition to the inner circle: Allicyn Hikida. She had been born and raised in Seattle, but moved to Hawaii to work for a local radio station. She was now with a private company in charge of their public relations and served on the board of directors of the

165

Allicyn conferring with Steve at a JACL function, 1992.

Honolulu JACL. She had become indispensable. Be it a press conference, a fundraiser, or a public forum, she was always in the background, quietly doing what needed to be done. She never let a detail escape her.

At about the time we were preparing for the NDRB, Senator Inouye had proposed an amendment to the appropriations bill for the Defense Department that required the Officer Candidate School, War College, Command and General Staff College, and military academies to certify in writing that "appropriate measures have been taken to publish and enforce regulations which expressly prohibit discrimination on the basis of race, color, religion, sex or national origin." Jennifer had worked on this legislation for months, and through her efforts our case was specifically named in the Senate–House conference report.

For years we had been ignored by the national press. However, the Tailhook scandal continued to unravel, placing the military increasingly under a microscope. A reporter for the *Dallas Morning News* was working on a story on

Speaking to supporters at the JACL fundraiser, 1992. Photo courtesy of *The Hawaii Herald*.

the problems with the military inspector general system. Another thick packet was sent. More long-distance phone calls. But this time the front page of the *Dallas Morning News* blared: "Military Inspectors Faulted: Critics Question How Military Handles Complaints." News of the story was slowly spreading beyond Hawaii.

We received more good news. General Carl E. Mundy, Jr., the new commandant of the Marine Corps, had ordered the formation of a quality management board led by Colonel David Vetter. Its purpose was to study the process of accessing and screening minority officer candidates into the Marine Corps. I could not help but believe that our case had contributed to the Marine Corps' recognition that minority candidates may not be receiving fair treatment at OCS.

On July 26, 1992, we held a fundraiser at the Japanese American Cultural Center of Hawaii. Local caterers donated Japanese and Hawaiian food. Flower shops provided the leis. A glossy newsletter with background on the case was printed. Gordon Kim, a childhood friend and professional musician, agreed to provide entertainment. With a large JACL banner in the background, I entered the room and was swept up in the moment. The aroma of the various foods filled the room. My entire family was there. Friends, old and new, were everywhere. There were politicians and journalists. The camera crews from local TV stations were working the crowd. The faces that brightened the room reflected a typical Hawaiian pallet of colors. The case had reached beyond the Japanese American community. With each passing day, it seemed to represent more than just discrimination. It was local boy against the U.S. government, a battle of the weak against the strong.

Our appearance before the NDRB in Washington, D.C., was less than four months away. In order to win, it was crucial to show that this case was not just an isolated incident. We had to show that there existed a pattern and practice of discrimination in the Corps. With time running out, we needed a smoking gun.

23

"Smoking Gun"

FALL 1992

W E METICULOUSLY BEGAN TO PREPARE OUR CASE.
I contacted Gabriel Vargas and Ronnie Catipon about testi-
fying before the NDRB. Vargas was eager to tell his story.
Catipon, although he agreed to appear, was less enthusiastic.
They would provide moving personal accounts of the 140th
OCS. Bill and Steve began a media campaign in hopes of
attracting interest by the national media in Washington.

We secured expert testimony to show that the racial
remarks had tainted the subjective leadership evaluation.
Dr. David Takeuchi, an early supporter of the case, set up
an interview with his colleague Dr. Stanley Sue, professor
of psychology and head of the Asian American Mental
Health Center at UCLA. Dr. Sue flew into Honolulu. He
had a professorial demeanor, but looked younger than I
expected. He presented to the inner circle academic
research showing that derogatory racial remarks can isolate
an individual and taint subjective leadership evaluations,
particularly when the remarks come from those in positions
of authority. He explained that since the 140th OCS staff
used derogatory racial remarks over the entire nine weeks,
it reinforced the stereotype that Japanese Americans are
"studious," "passive," " foreign," "sneaky," and/or the
"enemy." The competitive environment of OCS only exac-
erbated its harmful effects.

But most critically, we still needed to show a pattern of bias against minorities. I wrote to the Marine Corps, and under the Freedom of Information Act (FOIA), requested drop rates for minorities at OCS from 1982 to 1990. My experience with the FOIA, despite exacting regulations regarding compliance by government agencies, was that it was a crap shoot. I had sent many FOIA requests with varying results: sometimes voluminous documents were released, other times only a page or two; sometimes names were redacted or blacked out, other times they were not. It seemed to depend on who was assigned to process the FOIA, and that individual's particular mood that day. Like everything else, all I could do was wait.

We had been scheduled to appear on Thursday, November 19. The NDRB had no intention of making it easy. The responsibility to get witnesses to the hearing would be ours completely. Correspondence had flown back and forth between Clayton and the board, negotiating approval for the presence of observers and members of the press. "Space and security" would limit the number to twenty. Moreover, we had to provide the names and addresses of all individuals who planned to attend. Audio or video recording of the proceedings had been prohibited. There had been so many restrictions that Representative Abercrombie fired off a letter in protest. But the board had stuck to its guns.

The Marine Corps responded to our FOIA request. This time, there were reams of data. Of course, I knew that the accuracy of the data would only be as good as those doing the counting. Fortunately, when we looked over the numbers that had been gathered by the Marine Corps, we knew that it was significant. But we needed an expert to tell us why. Dr. Takeuchi came through again. He introduced us to James Dannemiller, president of SMS Research, a polling and statistics firm in Honolulu. Sporting an aloha shirt, he clearly knew his stuff. Together they had analyzed the figures, which covered an eight-year period and twenty-five

OCS classes. They wrote a report which concluded that there existed an "institutional bias against minority candidates at Officer Candidate School."

As I read the report I could not help but reflect on Eshelman. It appeared that the discrimination went far beyond just the 140th OCS. At best, it was tolerated, and at worst ordered by those at the highest levels of the OCS command. Ironically, it softened my view of him. After all, as a first lieutenant, he himself had been a wide-eyed OCS candidate only a few years earlier. I found it hard to believe that he could have let such unfairness continue unless he had received "guidance" from up the chain of command. Perhaps he was less guilty of discrimination, and more of ignoring his mandate to lead. As all of us have done at one time or another, he chose the path of least resistance. He went along to get along.

I was reminded that leadership starts at the top. Notably, the report looked at Colonel Reinke's tenure stretching over five classes between 1987 and 1989. The cumulative minority disenrollment rate under his leadership was 49 percent, which was 17 percent higher than for whites. The report noted that this was statistically significant, and that of the four colonels who had been assigned to the OCS command during that eight-year period, Colonel Reinke's record was the worst. They had found that in my class, the 140th OCS, there was a particularly strong relationship between race/ethnicity and graduation: 28 percent of the white candidates were disenrolled, while minorities had a whopping drop rate of 60 percent. This represented a rate that was 114 percent higher than for whites!

I remember putting down the report feeling vindication and hope. We had our smoking gun.

24

The Naval Discharge Review Board

NOVEMBER 19, 1992
MORNING

BEFORE I KNEW IT, WE WERE WALKING THROUGH the front doors of the NDRB, creating quite a scene. We had traveled to Arlington, Virginia, just outside Washington, D.C. Except for Dannemiller, we must have looked like a group of Japanese *salariman*. The startled sailor at the reception desk directed us to the elevator. I was a nervous wreck. Clayton was pure confidence.

As we exited the elevator on the ninth floor, members of the JACL—Washington, D.C. chapter and other observers were waiting in the hallway. I just smiled and nodded to everyone. I then noticed Eric Schmitt of the *New York Times*, John Lancaster of the *Washington Post*, and Chet Leonard from *Gannet News Service*. This was no accident. Bill and Steve had sent press releases, with repeated follow-up phone calls. Vargas had arrived. But Catipon had not. Lieutenant Colonel Goble led us to the hearing room, with the observers and media trailing behind.

The room resembled a courtroom with flags and plaques displayed on the walls. There were chairs in the back of the room for observers. Clayton, with his now familiar limp, marched up to a large conference table in the front, our backs to the observers. I followed behind him and we both took our seats. Facing us on the opposite side of the table were the

Inside this building was the Naval Discharge Review Board.

board members: Colonel Campbell, USMC; Colonel Smith, USMC; Lieutenant Commander Armstrong, U.S. Navy; and Lieutenant Colonel Goble. Colonel Aileen Albertson, USMC, the chairperson, called the proceedings to order promptly at 9 A.M.

"Good morning . . . the board is now open."

She was older with an air of sophistication. Take away the uniform and I could easily have imagined her being a professor at a local university. Most important, she seemed to be fair and reasonable.

I looked behind me to find a room packed with observers. But still no Catipon. I slumped in my chair. We hadn't even begun, and had already lost our first witness. Colonel Albertson reiterated that the board did not have the authority to delete any reference to unsatisfactory leadership or to reinstate me into the Corps. Clayton stated that he understood the board's limited authority, but would focus on two issues:

- Whether the racial harassment and discrimination tainted the evaluation that caused Mr. Yamashita's disenrollment.
- Whether there was a concerted effort by the noncommissioned officers at the 140th OCS to discriminate against minority candidates that was known and condoned by their superior officers.

It was time to call our first witness. Out of nowhere, Catipon appeared. Still out of breath, he barely had time to take off his coat. Lieutenant Colonel Goble asked him to raise his right hand, and he was sworn in. While I had been one of the oldest candidates, he had been one of the youngest. He had entered OCS right after college. He was six feet tall and 180 pounds. His parents were from the Philippines; he had been born and raised in Cleveland. He was now working as a defense analyst in the private sector, and was engaged to be married. I knew he was a reluctant witness.

Catipon testified that at the end of OCS he and Webster, a white candidate, both had failed the endurance run. Colonel Reinke had allowed Webster to retake it, while he had been immediately disenrolled. Clayton asked a few more questions and then turned it over to the board members.

"After all that you have been through, would you still recommend OCS to a young man coming out of college?" asked Lieutenant Commander Armstrong, a black officer and the only minority on the board. Remembering Brice, I could not help but be fearful of him.

174

"Yes, even if you do fail, it's how you accept that failure that shapes you as you grow older; you pick yourself up and try to learn from that . . . It was a good experience."

The board members were nodding; a few could not hide their glee. I'm sure they wished that I had taken my disenrollment more like Catipon. The questions continued for another 20 minutes. Finally, Lieutenant Colonel Goble tried to explain why Webster was given a second chance. He asserted that Catipon's overall PT performance would have made it difficult for him to pass the endurance run.

Clayton and I had met with Lieutenant Colonel Goble the day before. He was the board's recorder and the most experienced with procedures. He was stocky and physically intimidating. But most memorable was his voice. It was gravelly and slow in pitch. He had greeted us with a receptive smile, and had shown us to a room, where he allowed us to review the administrative record. As we left he had assured us that the hearing would be nonadversarial. I would soon learn that nothing could have been further from the truth.

Catipon sat there in silence, clearly wrestling with Goble's explanation of why Webster had been given a second chance. For the past few years he had blamed himself for his disenrollment. I fidgeted in my chair. He looked down at the floor, before finally looking up.

"All I know is that you have to be fair to everybody," he exclaimed, looking straight at Goble. Catipon was not the strongest witness. But he was articulate and sincere. Most important, his experience represented another example of unfair treatment at OCS. And in that moment I sensed that even he realized that something had gone terribly wrong at the 140th OCS.

Vargas was an impressive figure on the witness stand. His broad shoulders filled out his dark suit. No longer an officer candidate, he looked very much the yuppie businessman. Born in Bolivia, he had come to America as a child. He had let his dark brown hair grow out, and was slimmer and handsomer than I had remembered. Vargas was working in the high-tech industry, but unlike Catipon, felt that he had been mistreated. Clayton began by asking whether the staff had a physical stereotype of a Marine officer.

"That was pretty clear," Vargas answered immediately.

Clayton leaned forward in his chair before asking him to elaborate. Vargas testified that although the staff continued to harp on his physical appearance, they would not specify the deficiency. He had asked Sergeant Carabine point-blank, "Is it because I look more Hispanic than Anglo?" In response, Carabine had merely pointed to a picture on a wall. Clayton asked him to describe the picture.

"It was a Marine officer in dress blues on a recruiting poster, very Anglo, blond hair, blue eyes . . . I said that I don't look like that . . . I may never look like that."

Vargas testified that Carrabine ended the conversation, leaving him to "read between the lines." The board appeared unmoved.

Vargas went on to describe his platoon sergeant billet, which required him to work side by side with the platoon guide, a white candidate. He was shocked when Gunnery Sergeant Pitts gave him an unsatisfactory evaluation while he gave the white candidate an outstanding one. On another occasion, Brice inexplicably ordered him to stop doing push-ups during the combat conditioning course, which caused him to fail the overall event.

Clayton asked whether there had been a preselection as to which candidates would be booted out of OCS. Vargas

175

thought there had been. Clayton asked which candidates had been preselected.

"A lot of the minorities . . . and candidates that didn't have this physical appearance . . . I tried to overlook it, but it became apparent that there was a preselection process."

176 Vargas continued to relate his experiences and the details of his disenrollment. Clayton asked why he thought he had been kicked out.

"The Marine Corps will tell you its because of leadership; after looking back I don't agree that I was not a qualified officer candidate; I just don't believe that anymore . . . there were too many inconsistencies."

"Do you think your ethnic background . . . Hispanic background . . . had something to do with it?"

There was a brief pause as Vargas collected his thoughts while looking down at the floor. His eyes became misty.

"Sadly, I believe it had something to do with it; the fact that I didn't look Anglo; at some point I was targeted. I was to be documented and made to look on paper that I didn't have what it took to be an officer of Marines."

Questions were opened to the board. But it was clear that the board would not be an unbiased panel, but an agent of the Corps trying to discredit the case.

"Until you indicated you were Hispanic I would have sworn that you were of Irish descent," insisted Colonel Campbell, a tough-looking female officer. I heard groans coming from the observers. I sat there thinking it was an odd statement.

"But my last name, Vargas, is not Anglo, and at OCS you are always addressed by your last name," he responded with a hint of surprise.

"As you were sitting there you sure looked Italian to me," chimed in Colonel Smith, a wiry Marine with brownish hair. There were a few chuckles from the board and louder groans from the back of the room. I sat there incredulous. For over three years I had been working to get the

Marine Corps to take my allegations seriously. It seemed they still viewed it as a joke. Goble started his questioning. His friendly demeanor had disappeared. He pressed the issue on how Vargas had rated me on the peer evaluation.

"How did you rate Candidate Yamashita, please?" his voice filled with confidence.

Vargas sat there trying to remember. He fidgeted in his chair.

"Toward the bottom," he conceded.

Goble was trying to show that the racial remarks had nothing to do with my disenrollment, for even Vargas had thought that I was a screw-up.

"Why . . . did you rate him that way?" he insisted as the pace of his questioning quickened.

"Due to performance . . ."

"What was in his performance that would place him low?" Goble continued to press.

"What was it about Mr. Yamashita's performance that gave you doubts?"

"Um . . . um . . . I can't . . ."

"Mr. Vargas, what was it about his performance, please answer the question!"

Vargas was rattled. My stomach was churning. Goble leaned forward in his chair. Vargas struggled to collect his thoughts.

"Well . . . um . . . there was so much pressure put on Bruce Yamashita by the staff. It was hard to put your finger on how much was his fault, and how much was brought on by the staff . . . and that was a problem in evaluating Bruce."

I learned back in my chair. But Goble continued to press. He reminded Vargas that he had been ordered to rate me based on what he thought, not on what the OCS staff thought.

"Are you now saying you didn't do that?" Goble said accusingly.

"No, I did what I thought," countered Vargas.

"Even then you rated him in the bottom three, isn't that correct?" Before Vargas could answer he continued, "And the other candidates in the bottom three, did they graduate?"

Goble had made a basic mistake on cross examination: don't ask a question unless you know the answer.

"Yes . . . two of the three rated at the bottom graduated from OCS," Vargas shot back.

Goble knew that they were all white, which only confirmed the essence of our case. Vargas had weathered the initial attack. But Goble wasn't finished. His next line of questioning pushed the boundaries of relevance. He got Vargas to concede that he had an American ethic toward failure.

"So would it surprise you that it is difficult to accept failure? I know that I have a hard time accepting that I am at fault; I do a pretty good job rationalizing the reasons . . . ," said Goble, who had a tendency to punctuate his questioning with short asides.

"Is that a question or a statement?" objected Clayton as he rose in his chair.

"No, that's just a statement by me . . . an observation," Goble said, interrupting Clayton.

He continued grilling Vargas. He pointed out for the record that Vargas had been a marginal candidate. He noted his poor evaluation for his platoon sergeant instructor billet. He reminded him that at the last company inspection he was cited for a dirty rifle. Vargas appeared to be tiring. Clayton leaned forward in his chair and requested a break. Goble insisted on finishing.

"Would it surprise you to know that a candidate received an integrity chit for lying to a sergeant instructor, but was kept in training?" said Goble as he glared at me from across the table.

I knew where Goble was going. He was setting the stage for questions on the integrity chit that I had received from Brice. Clayton gave me a look of apprehension. All eyes of the board were on Vargas. He hesitated before he spoke.

"I question that . . . because there were instances where they questioned my own integrity . . ."

The hearing took on the ebb and flow of a trial, momentum swinging from one side to the other. Finally, Clayton rose to refocus the questioning.

"Mr. Vargas, what was the name of the sergeant instructor that questioned your integrity?"

"Staff Sergeant Brice"

Clayton skillfully paused to let the significance of that answer sink in. Vargas was exhausted, and so was I. I gave him a thumbs-up as he exited the room and headed for the elevator. There was a short recess. I noticed that the three reporters had left. My heart sank as the most important testimony was yet to come.

The Pressure Mounts

At 1200 hours Clayton called Dr. Sue to the stand. The board couldn't ignore his credentials. We wanted to convince them that the racial remarks had tainted the subjective leadership evaluation. He began his testimony by citing case studies going back to the turn of the century which showed the negative impact of racial slurs. Clayton then asked Dr. Sue his opinion as to whether there was bias at the 140th OCS.

"Well, you have candidates that state that the evaluation could have been biased, the record shows that there were racial remarks hurled at Mr. Yamashita, academic research indicates that racial slurs can bias individuals, and finally the Dannemiller/Takeuchi report. I can't see how you can come up with any other conclusion except that there was bias," said Dr. Sue matter of factly.

Commander Armstrong, with his broad shoulders and dark blue Navy uniform asked why there had been no blatant slurs against African American or Hispanic American candidates at the 140th OCS. Dr. Sue explained that the general public has been sensitized to those groups because of their larger populations and history of fighting for civil rights. He asserted that the sergeants would have been "crucified" if they had made similar slurs to an African

American. But such remarks toward an Asian American were still viewed as harmless. He concluded that Asian Americans, often considered not just as the model minority, but the silent one, would continue to suffer discrimination unless they began to organize and protest.

Colonel Campbell leaned forward in her chair, indicating to Colonel Albertson that she had a question. **181**

"It struck me about possible bias against Oriental people, and it would seem to me that the Marine Corps is probably the least likely place for that to happen since every Marine in this room has been to the Far East; many of our Marines are married to Orientals: Koreans, Filipinos, Japanese . . ."

I could hear the groans coming from the back of the room. The statement was irrelevant and patronizing. To make matters worse, the Asian American community has long considered the term "Oriental" as offensive. Colonel Albertson raised her hand to quiet the observers. Dr. Sue reminded Colonel Campbell that, regardless of what she thought, the IG investigation had verified that derogatory remarks were made at the 140th OCS. Goble moved to another line of attack. He condescendingly asked Dr. Sue if he had done any research on "controlled stress." Before Dr. Sue could finish, Goble cut him off, not with a question, but a speech.

"Well, I want to talk about controlled stress. . . . One of the main responsibilities of a Marine officer is to lead troops in combat. For a Marine officer the decision he makes will condemn somebody to die. You give me your children into my Marine Corps; I have the responsibility of them living or dying. Part of controlled stress is to find the Achilles' heel. Mr. Yamashita's Achilles' heel was that he was Japanese American. My concern is that sometimes minorities do things that flag their ethnicity. I personally don't have a problem with the bowing . . . I served four tours in the Far East and was a member of the Japanese American Friendship Society. But here you have a young man who had studied for four years at Georgetown University, lived in DC, shows up at OCS, and then bows?!"

Clayton jumped out of his seat.

"You're assuming that Mr. Yamashita did in fact bow . . . which is something that we will not concede . . . he will testify that he didn't bow!"

"Evidence presented has statements that he did bow . . . are you now saying that the evidence you submitted is not correct?" fired Goble.

All pretense of civility was gone. Pent-up frustration was finally boiling over.

"When we submitted the evidence we submitted the good and the bad . . . statements from Runyun, Brice, Eshelman, Winter . . . certainly not unbiased individuals . . . but we submitted it to make the record complete," said Clayton angrily.

Colonel Albertson tried to regain order.

"I don't think it makes any difference one way or the other. . . . Colonel Goble, you can pose it in the hypothetical, please," as she shouted over both Goble and Clayton.

"I don't think bowing is that important . . . particularly in light of all the racial slurs that were present," interrupted Dr. Sue.

It was a free-for-all. Colonel Smith jumped in to argue that even though there were slurs, the peer evaluations could not have been tainted because the candidates knew each other. The debate went back and forth. As I listened, I forgave Clayton for all the times I found him to be argumentative and difficult. He was doing a terrific job.

Colonel Albertson had the last question for Dr. Sue. Her calm demeanor seemed to settle everyone down.

"Instead of racial slurs in the mess hall, what if we said, 'you lawyers are all the same, why don't you go back and rip off the public' . . . do we now get into lawyers are being picked on?"

"If that sort of slur was made we would not be here

today," said an exasperated Clayton, leaning back in his chair, arms crossed, shaking his head.

Colonel Albertson's question revealed how different our perspectives were. As Dr. Sue looked across the table, his eyes watered with emotion.

"The history of race relations is not that you make fun of a profession; instead, it is a history of violence, the violence we see today in Los Angeles; that is not something we should be playing around with. Maybe centuries from now we can kid each other about ethnicity; today race is the single greatest problem in America."

There was silence from both sides of the table. I felt as if I had just gotten off a roller coaster ride. I looked down at my watch. It was 1:06 P.M.

"Does this board have lunch?" inquired Clayton with a slight smile.

Chuckles from the board helped release the tension.

"Welcome to a Marine Corps function. . . . we don't eat lunch," quipped Goble.

For our sake, the board recessed for lunch.

26

My Chance to Be Heard

Dr. Sue rushed off to National Airport to catch a flight back to L.A. We walked over to Ballston Commons Mall to get a quick bite. The crisp autumn air felt good against my face. I was exhausted, and I hadn't even testified yet. I was next. To a large extent the success of the hearing depended on my testimony. My stomach churned. I could almost see Colonel Goble chomping at the bit. I ate a banana and sipped some bottled water. Clayton gave last-minute advice.

We returned at 1400 hours. Clayton methodically led me through my testimony as I painstakingly described the twelve exhibits that we had submitted to the board. He then asked me about whether Staff Sergeant Brice had ever given me an integrity chit.

"Yes . . . he ordered me to write an essay. When he asked me to get it, I pulled it out of my locker and wrote my name on it before turning it in."

"And then what happened."

"Sergeant Brice went crazy . . . accused me of lying and gave me an integrity chit."

Goble shook his head and looked down at the table. He knew that the IG had determined that Brice had violated sections of the Equal Opportunity Manual. In his cross examination he didn't ask questions about the integrity chit. I can only assume he had wisely decided not to pit my credibility against that of Brice.

Clayton then asked me about the various incidents of derogatory racial remarks and unfair treatment. I stood up and placed two charts on an easel. The first chart listed the various allegations that had been submitted to the IG, and whether they had been substantiated, partially substantiated, or not substantiated. The second chart showed the distribution and frequency of remarks and incidents at OCS. The result was a rising curve, peaking at the ninth week.

With Clayton's prompting, I maintained that this ongoing, unlawful conduct had tainted the subjective leadership evaluation. I argued that there had been a conspiracy among the drill instructors and the officer corps that allowed the racial harassment. Clayton asked why I felt there had been a conspiracy.

"This was not one isolated incident . . . these incidents occurred over the entire nine weeks of the course, and at no point did the officer corps say, 'Don't do it'; when this happens it can only mean one thing: the officers knew."

I looked at the board and told them that I was an American. I spoke about the sacrifices of my grandparents and my parents, who each in their own way had made their contribution to America. I spoke about the internment and the 442nd Regimental Combat Team. I could feel myself being overcome with emotion. I tried desperately to control myself.

"Take a look around this room; we all look different."

Suddenly my voice cracked. All the pent-up frustration and anger came spewing forth. I needed time to compose myself.

"This is important not just to Bruce Yamashita, but to us all. Being an American has nothing to do with the color of your skin . . . it's an attitude, it's a spirit . . . ," I said, with my voice rising.

There was a long, uncomfortable silence. Colonel Campbell mercifully changed the subject by asking about my initial decision to make a complaint to the commandant. I had explained this many times before to other groups. I was on auto-pilot. She finally asked why I didn't accept the commandant's initial offer to reenter OCS and compete for a commission. I told her that I had finished OCS, and reminded her that the Marine Corps had broken the law.

"I don't think there's any evidence that laws were broken," insisted Colonel Campbell, trying to resume her attack.

I was baffled. How could a colonel in the Marine Corps, in light of all the evidence, make such a statement? The IG had found unequivocally that regulations had been violated. Clayton rose in his chair.

"Excuse me, is it the position of the board that violation of the Marine Corps Equal Opportunity Manual is not a violation of the law?"

"Yes," insisted Colonel Campbell.

I looked at Clayton. Colonel Albertson took a deep breath.

"Violation of the regulation is a violation of the law," interrupted Colonel Albertson in a slow voice. "But this board hasn't established that in fact laws were broken," she continued in an effort at damage control.

"That's what I was trying to say, but didn't say it as accurately as I should," said a clearly embarrassed Colonel Campbell.

Commander Armstrong did nothing to dampen my growing confidence or slow our momentum. My fears that as an African American he might be against me were unfounded. He tossed me a series of softball questions. He asked me whether I knew about the long history of discrimination in America. He spoke proudly of *Brown v. the Board of Education, Korematsu v. U.S.,* and other landmark civil rights cases. While the rest of the board denied any possibility of discrimination, Commander Armstrong seemed to imply that he was not surprised, and that indeed it might be rampant.

Now it was Goble's turn. This was his final shot at me. As far as he was concerned, my disenrollment had nothing to do with the racial remarks and unfair treatment. I was simply a screw-up. He reminded me of comments that I had written in my essays. I wrote of being depressed because of the stress that had been placed on me. He hammered away, implying that this had been the cause of my failure. He continued to pepper his questions with the words "depressed" and "depression," attempting to imply mental instability. The tension in the room went up a notch. He reminded me that I had injured my shoulder on the obstacle course, and had gone to sick bay for a groin pull.

"The time you spent in sick bay; you were there for two days on light duty, and five days in sick bay; here's a guy who is not pulling his weight," he said, with his voice rising.

He was grabbing at straws. My confidence was growing. Nobody knew this case better than I.

"Well, how do you explain Kempster, a white candidate who was in sick bay and on light duty for weeks and graduated?" Before Goble could answer I continued.

"Colonel Williams said he would look into it, yet it was not mentioned in the IG report. How do you explain that, Colonel Goble?" I said, looking straight at him.

Instead of an answer, he continued his attack.

"I'll be blunt with you. The question is with or without the racial comments would you have cut it. You are convinced that you would, but having been a Marine for thirty years . . . I AM NOT!"

He offered one final explanation for my disenrollment.

"Isn't it true that you had nothing in common with your classmates, and it wasn't about race, but life experiences; you could not bond with them . . ." I knew where Goble was going. I was offended. This time I cut him off.

"I think we had a lot in common. We were all Americans; we all wanted to serve our country; we wanted to be with the best. You find common ground, Colonel Goble . . . you don't have to all be the same to form a team. I have worked with people of different ages, ethnicities, and even languages, but we always found common ground," I thundered.

188

There was silence in the room. Colonel Albertson called for a 10-minute recess.

It was getting late in the day. Our final witness, James Dannemiller, was our anchor man. He explained the statistical approach used to analyze the numbers. Much of the explanation went over my head. He then presented the Dannemiller/Takeuchi report and a number of charts that graphically depicted the minority drop rates at OCS between 1982 and 1990. He concluded that race had been a factor not only in my disenrollment, but in the disenrollment of other minorities who had gone through OCS during that eight-year period.

Dannemiller then moved to the bigger picture. He spoke about the 1989 Military Equal Opportunity Assessment (MEOA). He concluded that it showed an ongoing problem with bias against minorities and women, not just at OCS, but in the entire Marine Corps.

I could see that the board did not like what it was hearing, but sensed that they were beginning to tire with all the numbers and charts. Colonel Campbell asked a few questions. Goble jumped in as well. The questions went round and round. Dannemiller took over the hearing with answers that were thorough and convincing. At times, it appeared that he was speaking to a class rather than providing testimony.

Colonel Albertson argued that statistics can be misleading because it doesn't take into consideration whether, for example, women are leaving the Corps due to marriage or pregnancy.

"And that's why this MEOC is inadequate. If I were the

boss trying to make the system work better, I'd throw this back hard 'cause I have nothing to work with here. I can't change anything with this!" he said, as he held the 2-inch-thick booklet, and in dramatic fashion pretended to throw it away.

Colonel Albertson pressed Dannemiller. She argued that the statistics were not that bad. There was a pause in the questioning as she flipped through the pages of statistics. She finally looked up.

"Well, for example, in the 140th OCS, I see 28.5 percent white dropout rate, and only a 31.5 percent minority drop rate; that's only a 3 percent difference," she remarked.

Danemiller seemed confused as he shuffled through his notes. I looked at Clayton.

"I beg your pardon, Colonel. The dropout rate for whites was 28.45 percent; the drop rate for minorities was 60 percent!"

There was another long pause as she once again studied the statistics. Finally, she raised her eyes back toward Dannemiller.

"Oh, 31.5 is the difference; I see, so it was a 60 percent drop rate . . . THAT IS HIGH."

She looked down at the table and let out a quiet sigh. Dannemiller had done his job. I had nothing more to say.

27

The Floodgates Open

LATE NOVEMBER 1992

THAT NIGHT WE CELEBRATED AT SARIS' NEW Orleans House, a half block away from our hotel. We were proud of ourselves. There was a feeling of accomplishment and camaraderie. After so many months and years of disappointment and frustration, we savored the moment. We tore into the huge buffet featuring slabs of roast beef. We ordered rounds of beer. We laughed into the evening, sharing the high and low moments of the day.

As we walked back to the Hyatt, Bill held out hope for national press coverage. He and Steve had worked on it for weeks. We knew the statistics would broaden the case's appeal. But we were still disappointed that the reporters had left so early. I thanked those who would be returning to Hawaii. I had declared the next day a personal holiday, and looked forward to walking over the Key Bridge to Georgetown. I made my way back to my room. I had left it in a mess; documents and charts were strewn all over the table and floor. The maid had changed the towels, but apparently left what she assumed to be organized chaos as it was. I took a shower and crashed.

At 6 A.M. I was awakened by the sharp rings of the telephone next to my bed.

I glanced outside my window into the darkness with one eye still closed.

"Well, you're on the front page of the *Washington Post!*" boomed Clayton, who was already at the airport. The article focused on the pattern of discrimination at OCS.

"Terrific!"

I was elated, but had no trouble going right back to sleep. The phone rang again. This time it was Bill.

"Congratulations! You made the *New York Times!*"

By now I was sitting up in my bed. The phone rang again. It was "Good Morning America." They invited me to appear on their show. By now both eyes were wide open. The rest of the morning was a blur. There were so many phone calls that the bellhop had to stuff phone messages under my door.

I spent the day giving interviews: *Chicago Tribune, Boston Globe, Los Angeles Times, San Francisco Examiner, Gannett News Service, Navy Times, AP,* CNN, and CBS News. Steve coordinated telephone interviews with the press back in Hawaii. Even members of the Japanese press showed up at my hotel door.

On Sunday, November 22, I flew to New York and checked into the Rhiga Royal Hotel for the "Good Morning America" appearance. This would be my first national interview. I appreciated all the work that had been done to bring us to this moment. I was fully aware that my performance would either help the case or hurt it. I called Steve from my hotel room.

"Don't worry. You're an old pro—just stick to the press points," he said in his usual reassuring voice.

The next morning at 6 A.M. a black limousine picked me up and drove me to ABC Entertainment. One of the assistants rushed me down a narrow corridor to a room where a makeup artist slapped on some foundation; then it was on to the Green Room, where I sat with several other guests. I recognized one of them as Joseph Califano, former heath, education and welfare secretary under President Carter. There were sandwiches, sesame seed bagels, fresh fruit, coffee, and juice. I couldn't eat. A TV monitor allowed us to watch the show. At the end of each segment, the next guest was introduced.

"Nobody ever said becoming a Marine Corps officer would be easy, but Bruce Yamashita never expected to find the racial abuse he says he received in officer training," said Charlie Gibson as he signed off for a commercial break.

All eyes slowly turned toward me. I gave them all a nervous smile. I was rushed into the studio.

"Just relax and look at Charlie when you're talking," the floor director instructed me.

This was live—with no chance to edit my mistakes. The pressure was intensified by the fact that I knew the Marine Corps would do all it could to discredit me. But all those interviews with the local Hawaii TV stations had given me valuable practice in telling my story.

The lights went on. Charlie Gibson asked me some easy questions and some tough ones. He then interviewed Colonel Vetter who was at Quantico, Virginia, via remote broadcast. I recognized him as the colonel who was charged with leading the quality management board investigation. As I sat there, even I couldn't help but be impressed with his perfect posture, olive green Service "A" uniform, and chest covered with colorful ribbons and medals. He was flanked by American and Marine Corps flags. Vetter stuck to the Marine Corps party line. But he did acknowledge, for the first time, that minorities were being disenrolled from OCS at higher rates than whites.

"We're concerned about that, and that is one of the issues we are exploring," he insisted.

The 10-minute segment was over before I knew it. And as efficiently as I had been escorted in, I was escorted out. The limousine picked me up at the studio door, and drove me back to the hotel. I immediately checked out and took a taxi through the Holland tunnel to Newark Airport.

That afternoon I had a meeting with the Marine Corps brass. They wanted to talk. I had heard rumors for months that there had been differences of opinion regarding the case. At least one general had been lobbying for the case to be resolved immediately. In light of the statistics of a pattern of discrimination, it had been his belief that it would be a mistake to brush the case aside. He had felt that if, left to simmer, it would prove to be embarrassing for the Corps. It had only been a rumor, but as I headed back to Washington the thought further boosted my spirits.

"I saw you this morning, Mr. Yamashita," said the ticket agent with a smile of support, as he handed me my boarding pass.

As I headed to the gate a college student gave me a thumbs-up. A few flight attendants came up to give words of support. A businessman stopped to shake my hand. I ducked into an airport cafeteria for breakfast. I noticed a TV monitor in the corner. As I worked my way down the cafeteria line, one of the workers, a large African American woman, recognized me.

"Yup, same old bullshit, ain't gonna end in my lifetime," she commiserated, shaking her head as she piled a mountain of scrambled eggs on my plate.

The words of support from total strangers gave me an indescribable sense of hope. As I boarded the plane I could not help but smile. The simple letter that I had sent to the commandant almost three years earlier voicing my protest had grown from a community issue in Hawaii to a national story. And more important, the case had touched an emotional chord, not just with the Asian American community, but with well-meaning Americans from across the country.

I landed in Washington, and headed for a meeting with the generals.

28

A Formal Offer

JANUARY 22, 1993

MARINE CORPS HEADQUARTERS IS IN THE NAVAL Annex, which stands on a hill overlooking the Pentagon. I had returned from New York and taken a taxi to meet with Brigadier General Gerald Miller, head of the Marine Corps Judge Advocate General Corps. It had been a busy weekend, but I was energized by the prospect of a resolution.

I called him from the security gate. While I waited for an escort, I observed crisp salutes by Marines and sailors as they passed each other. The escort led me into the massive building. After so many years of struggle, it felt surreal to finally be here. As we walked through the narrow, utilitarian corridors, the escort stopped to show me portraits of past commandants. Dressed in a coat and tie, I was shown into the general's office. He was tall and patrician in bearing. We chatted for a while; then he told me that his boss wanted to meet me. I followed him up the stairwell to the office of the deputy chief of staff for manpower and reserve affairs.

"Mr. Yamashita . . . nice to finally meet you!"

Waiting in front of the office was Lieutenant General Matthew Cooper. He was average in height with a warm smile, and had infantry written all over him. He shook my hand firmly, and invited me into his office. I could not help but be amazed that I was now speaking face to face with two generals. I had come a long way since my out-processing interview with Captain Garcia.

The Naval Annex.

Hiding my excitement, I calmly thanked both of them for taking the time to meet with me. Lieutenant General Cooper used the Washington Redskins as an ice breaker. I momentarily forgot where I was as we talked about the upcoming season. Then he moved on to basketball and the University of North Carolina Tar Heels. I waited for him to bring up my case.

Remembering my lunch with Lieutenant Colonel Brindle in Hawaii two years earlier, I was anxious to begin the discussion. I began by stating the need for the Marine Corps to revise its OCS SOP (Standing Operating Procedures), specifically in regard to the use of race to place stress on a candidate. They appeared to nod, but gave no definitive response.

Then the conversation moved to an appropriate remedy. I was asking for a retroactive commission, service credit, and back pay. Three years earlier, I had requested to be commissioned and be placed on active duty in the Marine Corps. Now I was asking for an honorable discharge. My fight with the Corps had been long and bitter. I had come to the conclusion that with each passing year, the prospect of serving had become less and less viable.

However, I specifically told them that I'd be willing to serve on active duty, if the Marine Corps deemed it necessary for a retroactive commission. I anxiously waited for their response. Surprisingly, they didn't appear to have a problem with my proposed solution. But they did express doubts whether they had the legal authority to provide, in particular, a retroactive commission. But they promised to research it and contact me in a week.

196

General Miller and I walked back to his office. He maintained a polite distance, but I got the sense that he was sympathetic to the case. He graciously offered to have one of his Marines give me a lift back to Dupont Circle. I thanked him and followed my driver out of the building. The air outside was cold and crisp. I felt like I was walking on clouds. There seemed to be real light at the end of the tunnel.

I continued to spread the word and keep the pressure on. I made a quick trip to San Francisco to meet with Steven Chin, a reporter for the *San Francisco Examiner*. He wanted to do an in-depth article for their Sunday *Image* Magazine. We spent the weekend shooting hoops and hanging out. The article, entitled "A Matter of Honor," would be published the following spring, and win a national award for excellence in journalism.

Rebecca Peterson, a producer for "60 Minutes," was considering the possibility of a segment on racism in the Marine Corps. Once again I sent stacks of documents. We spoke numerous times on the phone as she tried to assess the story.

The NDRB had made a decision. Not unexpectedly, it found, in denying the petition, that the relief requested was "not within the jurisdiction of the board." But our personal appearance had brought national attention to the case, and had moved it, for all practical purposes, beyond the NDRB.

The mood in the inner circle was hopeful. The Marine Corps had promised to contact me in a week, but two weeks passed without a word. Every morning I picked up the phone and dialed General Miller's number, only to hang up at the last moment. I reminded myself to be patient. Four weeks, still no word. All I wanted to hear was one word, "YES!" Over a month after our meeting, I called General Miller.

"A retroactive commission is not legally possible. However, Lieutenant General Cooper will contact you with a counteroffer."

I hung up the phone. It was a disappointment. But I knew that inherent in any negotiation is that each side does not get all that it wants. I remained hopeful that they would at least address our other demands. A week later General Miller notified me that the counteroffer would be sent directly to Assistant Secretary of the Navy Barbara Pope for her approval. There was no discussion. It would be a unilateral decision. He told me that the formal offer would be sent the week of January 4, 1993.

I returned to Hawaii in time for the holidays. It had now been almost four years since my disenrollment. The fact that the Marine Corps still had not provided a formal offer put a damper on our New Year's Eve party. But the efforts of the inner circle and others had allowed me to be selected one of the "Ten Who Made a Difference" by the *Honolulu Star-Bulletin*. The good news was that it kept the story alive and in the public's eye. Family and friends called to give words of encouragement. Maybe the new year would be a good one after all.

The week of January 4 came and went. A week later, I telephoned Lieutenant General Cooper. He apologized for the delay, and assured me that he would be meeting with the commandant, and that a final settlement offer was imminent. Seeking the most favorable offer possible, I told him that a public commissioning ceremony, and changes to the OCS SOP, would improve the chances for a resolution.

"I have no problem with a public ceremony, but don't like you changing the OCS SOP. It seems you now have a different agenda!"

"General, I'd be less than honest if I told you my agenda was only to get a commission . . . it's just as important to ensure it never happens again," I replied firmly.

Cooper was right. Over the past few years my agenda *had* changed. The case was no longer just about a commission and returning to serve on active duty. If the Marine Corps was serious about nondiscrimination, then it would have to acknowledge the years that had passed since 1989. It would have to acknowledge that the racial harassment had tainted the evaluation process at OCS, and revise the OCS SOP. Perhaps most important, it needed to face the fact that it had a problem with regard to the accession, retention, and promotion of minority officers.

On Friday, January 29, Pop called to tell me that a letter from the Marine Corps had arrived. I hurried home and saw the letter lying on the dinner table. I slowly unsealed the envelope.

Dear Mr. Yamashita,

. . . We are not prepared to commission you retroactively. However, in order to afford you the benefit of the doubt, even though your successful completion of OCS and, thereby, your eligibility for a commission remain in question, we are prepared to request that the Secretary of the Navy authorize us to commission you a second lieutenant on or after April 1, 1993. The accompanying obligation is that you: (1) attend the Basic School (six months) immediately following commissioning; and thereafter (2) attend Naval Justice School (nine weeks) You could be released from active duty . . . as early as December 21, 1993 with a Reserve obligation of six years. . . .

Sincerely,
M. T. Cooper
Lieutenant General
U.S. Marine Corps
Deputy Chief of Staff for
Manpower and Reserve Affairs
January 22, 1993

My initial reaction was disappointment. There was no retroactive commission, and the tone of the letter was unapologetic. And yet, as I held the letter in my hand, I could not help but be incredulous. The mighty Marine Corps had reversed its position, and was actually offering to commission me. The case had come a long way since that terse letter from Commandant Gray stating that "Yamashita is looking for reasons outside of himself to fault . . ." I stood there alone, savoring the moment. I read the letter again and again.

Now I had to make the difficult decision whether to accept it.

Standing Firm

Dear Mr. Yamashita,

Since our telephone conversation, I have personally reviewed the current OCS SOP and determined that additional revisions are necessary. A new revision has been prepared and will be incorporated in the SOP. . . . My staff will forward you a copy of the revision as soon as the SOP has been officially updated. Should you decide to accept a commission, Gen. Mundy will commission you at an appropriate ceremony in Senator Inouye's office.

Sincerely,
M. T. Cooper
Lieutenant General, U.S. Marine Corps
February 4, 1993

When it rains it pours. I looked at the three pages of revisions to the OCS SOP. They directly addressed incidents of racial discrimination and unfair treatment. They even added a section that included strong language prohibiting sexual harassment. I wrote a letter to Lieutenant General Cooper commending the revisions. If nothing else came of the case, but these revisions, the Marine Corps was the better for it. The offer to have the commandant of the Marine Corps commission me at Inouye's office was amazing.

On Wednesday February 17, the inner circle met. Clayton

argued in favor of accepting the offer and allowing him to litigate the retroactive commission. A part of me agreed with Clayton. But Ernie cautioned that any legal settlement would require me to waive my right to pursue any other action against the Corps. The rest of the group had mixed emotions. But in the manner of an experienced trial lawyer, Clayton hammered his point home.

"Just remember, Bruce, if you reject this offer . . . you may never be a Marine."

That night I had dinner with Jennifer at a local Japanese restaurant. She was now running the local office, and her priority was to rehabilitate the senator after the bruising 1992 campaign. More than ever she had become crucial to the case. Although ostensibly she was just my liaison to the senator, I suspected that as the years had passed her power and influence over the case had grown.

I showed her the letter. I felt that the Marine Corps had reneged on their initial agreement, which had included a retroactive commission, provided they had the authority. This letter didn't even address whether or not they could legally provide a retroactive commission. For the first time, I saw a hint of frustration. She made it clear that the senator would not push the case any farther.

A customer seated at another table sent over two large bottles of beer. He then stood up and walked over to our table. "I've been following your case . . . we're behind you . . . go for it!"

Jennifer pretended not to be impressed. Then our conversation shifted to a lighter topic. Over the beer we reminisced about Georgetown.

"Yeah, of all the Hawaii girls you were the smartest, prettiest, and had the best personality," I said mischievously.

"All right, I'll talk to the senator about a retroactive commission," she said with a smile and a hint of exasperation.

I was like a used car salesman, perfectly willing to grovel to close the deal. I seized the opportunity, and argued that I could sell the present offer to the JACL, but there would be those who would grumble. The senator had spent so much political capital on the case that for him to do less than go all the way would be a waste. Jennifer reluctantly agreed.

"I'll talk to him . . . hopefully we can make a final announcement in March."

The Marine Corps wanted a decision. We stalled for time by acknowledging receipt of Lieutenant General Cooper's letters and promising a reply by April 1. A few weeks later, I wrote another letter requesting a response with regard to whether the Marine Corps had the authority to provide a retroactive commission. This request effectively pushed the deadline beyond April 1.

Jennifer increasingly became preoccupied with other issues in her office. I admit that I was becoming a pest. But securing an acceptable resolution had become an obsession. I did manage to schedule one final meeting with her. I asked Mike Tokunaga, a 442nd veteran and influential member of the Hawaii Democratic Party, to attend. The inner circle wanted me to impress upon Jennifer the importance of the retroactive commission. Calling in Mike Tokunaga was a last-ditch effort to show that retroactivity was important to a lot of people, not just the JACL. He was physically big for a man of his generation, and gave the impression that he had gotten into his share of barroom fights in his youth. When we got to the senator's office located at the federal building in downtown Honolulu, he seemed to take over. He swaggered in and insisted that we meet, not in a conference room, but in the senator's empty office. The meeting was tense.

"I have been in public service for thirty-two years and whenever there is a reinstatement . . . retroactivity is AUTOMATIC," Tokunaga bellowed.

Then everyone turned toward me. I hesitated for a moment. I knew that Jennifer did not like what she was hearing.

"The Marine Corps has to come clean. If a retroactive commission is not legal, then they should state it. If it is legal, then they should be compelled to execute a retroactive commission. But they shouldn't be allowed to avoid the issue by simply saying 'we are not prepared' to provide a retroactive commission," I argued.

"All right . . . go talk with General Cooper . . . let me know what happens," she said, clearly aggravated.

I took this to mean that Senator Inouye would continue to support our efforts. The meeting had bought me time and hope. But three weeks later all the frustration of the past three years came to a head. Mike Tokunaga had told me that, according to Senator Inouye, the problem was that I didn't want to serve. I then called Jennifer.

"I think there has been a miscommunication. I'm willing to serve if the Marine Corps provides a retroactive commission."

"Are you accusing me of not doing my job!?"

I was a bit shocked at her response. For a moment I was not going to say anything, but emotion got the better of me.

"No, but it's been frustrating. Sometimes I wonder whose side you're on," I blurted.

"Well, that's not my style! These past few years have put a strain on our friendship!"

She slammed the phone down. I sat there feeling numb. Perhaps we didn't see everything eye to eye, but what I had said was dumb. After all, she had been my liaison to the senator. She had written letters, press releases, and legislation. She had spent countless hours tracking the case, and had given sound counsel. I hated the thought of losing a friend. I hated the thought of losing a crucial ally, and with it, any hope of convincing Inouye to stay with the case.

I was tired. A part of me wanted to claim victory and go home. I spoke with Bill every day to discuss the pros and cons. Ernie, Steve, and Allicyn had come to the conclusion that the offer was too little, too late. Their position was that we should reject it and fight on. But Clayton continued to argue that if I rejected this offer, the widespread support we had enjoyed could dissipate. Moreover, we would risk alienating Inouye, and be forced to fight the Marine Corps on our own. The discussion went back and forth. Heated arguments erupted.

204

But I was slowly coming to a decision. I had been fighting too long to accept a settlement that failed to address important principles of the case: the Marine Corps had to account for the years that had passed by providing a retroactive commission, concede that the racial remarks had tainted the evaluation process, and acknowledge that it had a problem with regard to procuring, promoting, and retaining minority officers. I appreciated Clayton's warning that if I refused the offer, I might never become a Marine. I fully realized that this could be my last best chance to claim victory. But in the end, knowing that we stood for what was right, I was willing to risk it all.

"We Were on Our Own"

TWO WEEKS LATER, MY DECISION MADE, I ATTENDED a JACL regional conference in Los Angeles. The National JACL would continue the fight. Congressman Neil Abercrombie pledged support for a resolution requesting a retroactive commission. I continued on to Washington to get a sense of other congressional support.

I met with Karen Narasaki, an early supporter, now serving as the executive director of the JACL—DC office. She had everything lined up. We first visited the office of Senator Daniel K. Akaka. He was Hawaii's "other senator." He came rushing out of his office to give me a warm Hawaiian hug; he reminded me how proud he was of the effort and pledged his support. I could always count on his aloha. To this day, he still seeks me out of a crowd to see how I'm doing.

The rest of the day we made the rounds: Congresswoman Patsy Mink, Congressman Norman Mineta, and Congresswoman Patricia Schroeder. They all assured me that they would support the resolution.

"If you accept, then it validates the Marine Corps' strategy to stonewall! It let's them give a straight commission, even years after the unlawful disenrollment, without penalty to them and with no compensation to the complainant," bemoaned one staffer.

The consensus was that with the newly elected Clinton

administration, and the ongoing Tailhook scandal, the timing was right to fight the Marine Corps all the way. Everyone predicted a whole slew of new civilian appointees at the Pentagon, who would be more sympathetic to civil rights issues. But they all agreed that if I wanted to continue the fight, then I needed at least the tacit support of Senator Inouye.

I understood that it was easy for the others to say fight on, while difficult for the senator to abandon the current offer. After all, he had lobbied and cajoled the Marine Corps behind the scenes. His position was that the current offer was acceptable, and that in politics you take what you can get. My unenviable task was to try to convince him otherwise.

But at this point getting a face-to-face appointment with the senator would be difficult. I felt that I could no longer go through Jennifer. She had done all she could do. I had no choice but to send a letter myself to ask for a meeting. The JACL made their request. Governor John Waiheʻe sent a letter. The senator agreed to meet me on April 19 at 3:30 P.M.

I arrived at the Hart Senate office building early. My heart was pounding. We all take action out of inspiration or desperation; this was desperation. I had brought a carefully wrapped gift. Bill had told me that the senator enjoyed Japanese *tsukudani*. I had spent a whole day running around Honolulu trying to find just the right brand. The senator had done a lot for me. I couldn't call on him empty-handed. At 3:25 P.M. I took a deep breath, and headed for the elevators up to the office. His aide immediately showed me to a reception room with a couch and two chairs. The room had the flags of all five branches of the service and beautiful art objects tastefully displayed.

The senator appeared. He looked tanned and vigorous as he sat down. But he didn't smile, and appeared annoyed. I had become a thorn in his side. I presented him the *tsukudani,* which he acknowledged with only a nod. It was clear that he wanted to shut this case down. I thanked him pro-

206

fusely for all his help. I made it clear I was willing to honor my contract, which would include the Basic School, Naval Justice School, and six years' service in the reserves. All I expected was for the Marine Corps to honor their side of the contract, which would necessarily include a retroactive commission. He insisted that the current offer was good, and that he could not support the case any further.

"Senator, do you really think what they're offering is fair?"

"What is fair?" he responded rhetorically.

He spoke about the recent allegations of sexual misconduct against him during the last campaign with pain in his face. My body stiffened.

"Do you think that was fair!?"

I didn't answer. He argued that retroactivity could not be accomplished by legislation, or by the secretary of the navy or secretary of defense.

"And that is why we will be making a request to the president," I insisted.

He suddenly turned fatherly in his tone. He advised me that President Clinton would be reluctant to get involved in the case in light of all his problems with the military. He talked about Clinton's efforts to allow gays to serve in the military.

"Listen, take the offer," he said matter-of-factly.

For a moment I was ready to throw in the towel. It would be easier to say "yes" and make him happy. But I had come too far. I had sacrificed too much.

"Senator, don't you think a complete resolution of the case would set a good precedent?"

His face was expressionless. I was bracing myself to be thrown out of his office.

"Probably," he replied slowly.

I told him that the rest of the Hawaii congressional delegation were circulating a resolution reaffirming support for the case. Suddenly his face tightened.

"This case has come this far because of me . . . it took muscle and my muscle," he said, jabbing the air with his index finger.

"But it's not over yet. I still need your support," I pleaded.

208   "I am not gonna bullshit you. I cannot sign the resolution."

He explained that he had already thanked the commandant for the current offer. It was a done deal. The resolution would be a slap to the commandant's face. He continued to press.

"Just remember, if this issue reaches the White House, the president will call me. Not to drop names, but the president calls me often," he said.

There was a long silence. I took a deep breath.

"Well, Senator, I am not gonna bullshit you either . . . I've been doing this damn thing for almost four years. I will go forward with or without you . . . but my supporters and I need to know, if the president calls, what you will say?"

The senator glared at me. Finally, he responded, reluctantly.

"If he calls, I'll support your position 100 percent; I'll argue your case as if I were your lawyer; I'll say it's a good precedent to set."

He reminded me that what I was seeking was unprecedented. I could feel all the years of frustration boil over.

"We are not doing this, Senator, because it is going to be easy; if we had that attitude we would never have brought the case in the first place."

The meeting was coming to a close.

"Senator, I started this thing. I intend to finish it."

He closed the meeting saying that sometimes persistence can pay off. I slowly stood up, and shook his hand. He thanked me for the *tsukudani*.

"If you get your retroactivity will you serve?" he asked, looking me straight in the eye.

"Absolutely," I replied looking straight back.

I picked up my briefcase, and straightened my shoulders. I could feel the staring eyes of the secretary as I marched out. I had accomplished what I set out to do. But I sensed that it was less a case that I had won the senator over, and more that I had secured an assurance that he would not get in our way. I had this sinking feeling that, from here on in, we were on our own.

31

The Commandant Speaks

SUMMER/FALL 1993

REBECCA PETERSON OF "60 MINUTES" CALLED TO request an on-camera interview in Washington. It was going to be at the Grand Hotel on M Street. The program would reveal a pattern of discrimination not just at OCS, but also in the promotion of minorities in the officer corps. I walked into the large suite where the cameras and lights were set up. There was a stir among the crew as Lesley Stahl walked into the room and took possession of it as though it were a stage. She was pleasant to me, but less forgiving of the crew. When a cameraman requested a retake because he felt the camera angle was slightly off, she went into a tirade. He soon conceded that maybe the shot would be okay. She then calmly turned back to me with a smile. I had done many interviews, but never with quite the flair as this one. The interview was taped and ready to go. But this was show biz; they could still decide not to run the story.

On May 20, 1993, a little over four years since my disen-rollment, the JACL called a press conference to announce formally my rejection of the Marine Corps offer. Allicyn had become the newly elected president; her leadership meant a smooth transition for the case. We had spent weeks preparing. Unless it was carefully placed in context, the potential for misinterpretation was rife, and I could be attacked as an ingrate, or worse, a coward. If we lost public support, we would have little leverage to keep pressing the case. The JACL briefed the veterans, made arrangements to hold the news conference at Club 100, and surrounded me with decorated veterans of military service pounding home the message that to accept this offer would be wrong. A newsletter was printed stating our position and asking supporters to write the president. The inner circle braced itself for criticism.

"We may take a few hits, but overall we'll do just fine," said Steve, his "damn the torpedoes, full steam ahead" attitude as strong as ever. And he was right. Most of the community supported our decision. The few negative letters came from those who had been critical of the case from the outset.

We continued to get the story out to as many individuals and organizations as possible. In Washington I hit the lobbying trail: Organization of Chinese Americans, Asian Pacific American Labor Alliance, Asian Pacific American Law Students Association, Mexican American Legal Defense and Education Fund, National Association for the Advancement of Colored People (NAACP), National Council of La Raza,, Puerto Rican Coalition, American Civil Liberties Union, U.S. Commission on Civil Rights. I also spoke with Senators Bill Bradley and John Glenn; Congressmen Ron Dellums, Robert Matsui, Norman Mineta, Don Edwards; and reporters from the *Los Angeles Times, Chicago Tribune, New York Times,* and *Navy Times.*

By 1993 the booming bubble economy in Japan had burst. My jobs with the Japanese companies were beginning to dry up. Despite assistance from the JACL Legal Defense Fund, I still had racked up some personal and long-distance phone bills. Travel back and forth across the continent did not come cheap. Money was tight. But, at the last moment, some job would come through, providing much needed income.

June 26 was the JACL Honolulu chapter annual awards luncheon, which was attended by hundreds of supporters. I was honored with the Civil Rights Award, but more

Speaking at our press conference held at Club 100, 1993. Photo courtesy of *The Hawaii Herald*.

important, it was an opportunity to rally the troops. It was an extravaganza at the Sheraton Waikiki Hotel Ballroom, complete with light show and a video production chronicling the case. The media was there to cover the event. There were other awardees, including Olympic Gold Medalist Kristy Yamaguchi.

At about the same time the Marine Corps sent us the quality management board's final report. It concluded that the Marine Corps had difficulties procuring, promoting, and retaining minority officers, and that its affirmative action program was the weakest of all branches of the service. It noted that other services had plans that were "significantly more comprehensive, far reaching and aggressive." It confirmed what we had been saying from the beginning.

But soon the activity died down. Correspondence with the Marine Corps ended. My trips to DC were no longer necessary. The media stopped calling. Even the inner circle began to meet less frequently. It would be another long, hot summer to ponder if and when the case would end.

Bill and I share a quiet moment during the JACL annual awards luncheon, 1993.

In the meantime, we had to deal with another ongoing issue. The case had begun in Quantico, but was being fought 5,000 miles away in Hawaii. We had garnered grassroot support in Hawaii, but the legal, political, and media focus had shifted to the East Coast. The JACL would help me relocate. So in late September 1993, I made the difficult decision to move back to the Boston House in Washington, D.C.

I was comfortably settled in when Mother and Pop came through on their way home from a trip to Turkey. In their retirement they had enjoyed traveling the world together. I knew Mother would want to see and do everything, so I braced myself for the visit. As expected, she made the most of their stay, hitting all the attractions. Pop had been a good sport, but he looked old and frail. It had been precious time together. But I also felt a sense of sadness. Within a week of their return, Mother called to tell me that Pop's cancer had spread. I could hear the strain in her voice. The family tried to stay positive. He went in for further surgery on his cheek, which made it difficult for him to eat and speak. I felt a desperate urgency to resolve the case. If Pop was going to die, I wanted him to go in peace.

The "60 Minutes" segment would be aired Sunday, October 31. It had been scheduled the week before, but at the last moment had been postponed. We had notified everyone again, and had our fingers crossed that it would be a go. Bill, who was now attending law school in Washington, D.C., and his wife Reyna, came over to the Boston House to watch. She grabbed the recliner. Bill and I remained standing.

Lesley Stahl presented statistics from the Dannemiller/Takeuchi report and the MEOC. She interviewed me and minority Marine officers showing discrimination not just at OCS, but also in the promotion of Marine Corps officers. Her final interview was with the commandant of the Marine Corps: Carl E. Mundy, Jr.

"So what's going on?" she asked. The commandant looked confidently into the camera.

"The problem is that minorities don't shoot that well . . . they don't swim that well and when you give them a compass at night, they don't do well at that sort of thing either," he said.

The camera flashed back to Stahl, who appeared stunned. The next day civil rights organizations throughout the country expressed outrage. That evening Dan Rather on the "CBS Evening News" reported that the Pentagon had issued a formal apology for the commandant's remarks. The next day the commandant fired off a memo to the fleet stating that his remarks had been "taken out of context." Everyone related to the case felt that victory was imminent. But this had happened so many times before: progress, media attention, raised hopes, followed by inaction.

Then I received a call from the Pentagon.

32

"There Will Be No Ratcheting Up"

It was a cold December day, a little over a year since I had traveled this same route to meet with Generals Cooper and Miller. This time my taxi proceeded straight to the Pentagon, passing by Marine Corps headquarters. A sailor dressed in a dark enlisted winter uniform met me at the security gate, and escorted me through a series of narrow, winding corridors. He showed me to a reception area and invited me to sit down. The richness of the decor was the first sign that I had moved beyond the Marine Corps, up the chain of command to the Department of the Navy.

"Hi, Bruce. Thanks for coming!"

It was Frederick K. Y. Pang, tall, slim, and distinguished. His informality put me at ease. As newly appointed assistant secretary of the navy for manpower and reserve affairs, the department had made this case his top priority. I could not believe I was here talking to him; our many appeals to his predecessor had been unsuccessful. He showed me into his office. It was spacious and ornately decorated with plaques and flags. There was a large desk as well as a conference table, but he invited me to sit on a comfortable settee that was off to the side. He sat opposite me in a club chair with a low coffee table between us.

"Here, have some chocolate macadamia nuts," he said, placing a dish full of Hawaiian candy on the coffee table.

I had met him briefly a month earlier when he was a senior staffer for Senator Sam Nunn, chairman of the Armed Services Committee, but had not really had a chance to talk. This time was different, and I was reminded that life is full of coincidences. Secretary Pang was older, but he too had been born and raised in Hawaii. He had grown up in the Punchbowl area of Honolulu like my mother. He had attended Mckinley High School like Pop. He had attended the University of Hawaii like all of us kids. I told him that my grandfather had had a barbershop in the Punchbowl area for over forty years.

"Not old man Kaneshige? He used to cut my hair when I was a kid!" he exclaimed, as he rocked back in his chair with a smile.

A friend of mine has a favorite saying, "Success travels at the speed of relationships." Throughout the case, each individual, each board, each organization had to decide if I was a man of integrity, or, in the words of General Gray, "looking for reasons outside of himself to fault." For Assistant Secretary Pang, it was no different; he too would have to evaluate. Sometimes it takes years to get to know and trust someone. Sometimes it takes minutes. With Secretary Pang there was an instant connection. He knew who I was and where I came from.

Before I knew it an hour had passed. I sensed I was no longer speaking with the assistant secretary of the navy, but hanging out with Fred. It felt great, but there had been too many meetings with only small talk. I mentioned the time, but he was unconcerned. He had blocked out his entire afternoon for this meeting. I was impressed and appreciative. He was a busy man, but he didn't want our meeting to be rushed.

Eventually, the discussion turned to the case. He pulled out a draft letter with his proposed offer, and slid it on the coffee table toward me.

"Take a look at it, and tell me what you think."

I was amazed. Up until now it had been take it or leave it. It was a rare gesture of goodwill. I studied the letter. There was an acknowledgment of wrongdoing, and a proposed remedy: commission me at the rank of captain, which was an attempt to account for the years that had passed since 1989. But there were shortcomings: no back pay or service credit. Fred made it clear that the secretary lacked the authority. I pulled out a list of my requests and placed it on the table. I was requesting:

1. A statement that derogatory racial remarks tainted the subjective leadership evaluation.
2. An acknowledgment that the current administrative system is inadequate.
3. The opportunity for training and to be placed on ready reserve.
4. Backdating of commissioning date to April 14, 1989.

"I'll try my best . . . but as you know this is a joint decision by persons at the highest levels. The current offer has already been approved by the top lawyer and public affairs officer for the Navy, all the undersecretaries, and Secretary of the Navy Dalton."

"I'll rework the offer the best I can, but the next offer is the final one. There will be no ratcheting up," he warned. His face and voice became serious.

I glanced at my watch. We had been together the whole afternoon.

Over the next days, phone calls went back and forth between me and Hawaii. Two days later I called Fred, reiterating the reasons for our remaining requests.

On December 5, I returned to the Pentagon for our final meeting. The Marine Corps had refused to modify their original offer. Nevertheless, Fred had added language stating that the racially insensitive treatment to which I was subjected may have tainted my evaluations, and acknowledged that he was taking this special action because the current administrative system provides no other remedy. It was not all that I had wanted. Remembering my promise to Senator Inouye to serve, I renewed my request for Marine training, which would include the Basic School and the Naval Justice School, and to be placed on ready reserve status. This would have required me to serve one weekend a month, and two weeks on active duty over the summer. Fred stated that with the downsizing of the military, training and ready reserve status would not be possible. I would immediately be placed in the stand-by reserve, the lowest echelon of readiness. I needed to think about it. He wanted an answer by Christmas.

"Listen, I know it is none of my business, but take the high road if you can," he said.

I expressed my concern that if the offer became public I might be hounded by the press. He acknowledged that his office had received a number of inquiries, but promised the Navy would not say anything.

I raced out of the Pentagon, clutching Secretary Pang's letter.

33

Breakthrough

January 1994

I hailed a cab and raced to the Grand Hotel, where Clayton was attending a bar convention. We went across the street to a restaurant fronting M Street. It was lunchtime, but we were able to grab a corner table. I showed Clayton the letter. He was ecstatic, particularly with the statement that the current system did not provide any other remedy.

"And there's no statement preventing you from pursuing further legal action—incredible!" he exclaimed.

We rushed back to his room. We were afraid the Navy would leak the offer. I had visions of reporters descending upon us and demanding a response. Clayton suggested a preemptive strike by releasing the story first. I frantically tried to reach Steve. We left our number on his pager. Steve called back 30 minutes later, and seemed annoyed that Clayton would even suggest releasing the story. He ordered us to withhold comment, and to return to Hawaii immediately.

That afternoon Eric Schmitt of the *New York Times* called to inquire about any updates on the case. Twenty minutes later, Gidget Fuentes of the *Navy Times* called. This was no coincidence. I stalled.

"Come to the *Times* first," implored Schmitt, who had called back and hinted that he knew more than what he was letting on.

He pressed further. He wanted an exclusive. I didn't want to tell an untruth. I acknowledged that an offer had been made, but that I could not reveal the details or make a decision until after I returned to Hawaii. I promised to call him by Christmas.

220 I returned to Hawaii. Bill, Steve, and Allicyn were satisfied. The new offer addressed most of the important issues. Ernie was the last holdout. The only Marine of the group, he held the Corps to a higher standard. He still believed that the secretary of the navy could resolve the retroactive issue in one fell swoop. I understood his frustration. I assured him that the settlement would allow us to pursue the rest of our demands via the BCNR, and if necessary, federal court. Ernie was finally convinced. The inner circle was in agreement.

I called Fred just before Christmas. He was on vacation, so I left a message with his aide: I would be accepting the offer; and my acceptance letter would go out at the end of the week. The media was Steve's domain; he would coordinate the announcement of our acceptance. Hoping to get the broadest coverage, he selected Sunday, January 2, because the day after New Year's Day is traditionally a slow news day. Moreover, the Sunday paper has the highest circulation for the week. Allicyn made all the arrangements to hold the press conference at the Alana Hotel in Waikiki.

I ordered everyone to keep the offer under their hats. We were considering working with the *New York Times*, and we didn't want the story to be scooped up by the local press. On December 27, we began calling supporters to invite them to a press conference to announce a "major development." Schmitt assured us that if he got an exclusive, he would make sure it ran in the Sunday paper. Steve wanted to wait until the last possible moment to commit. On the morning of Friday, December 31, I called Schmitt to tell him of the offer and my decision to accept. We were confident that it would be too late for some unknown editor to slip it

Steve making the announcement, 1994.

into the Saturday paper. All other media were faxed the story early Sunday morning.

At 7 P.M., the night before the press conference, I was going over my acceptance speech. I couldn't help but reflect on the soundness of the inner circle's initial strategy: strong legal case, political pressure, media coverage, and grass-roots support. Each prong, standing alone, would not have been enough. But taken together, it created a synergy that proved to be the difference. Suddenly, the phone rang. It was Steve. He had called to tell me that the story had made the Sunday edition, which hit the streets of New York at 10:30 P.M. on Saturday. Apparently, he had coerced a friend to brave the winter cold, and buy a copy off the newsstand.

Sunday, January 2, 1994, was a sunny day with the trade winds blowing just enough to keep one cool. I got to the hotel a little late. Steve, with a cigarette in his hand, was pacing outside holding the *New York Times*. I walked inside and saw the faces that had supported the case for all these years. The family was there in full force. The only one I missed was Pop, who had been too weak to make it. The room was packed. I was covered with leis. The press had set up their cameras. No one knew what to expect. The inner circle had kept the secret.

Steve stepped up to the podium. He announced that it had been almost five years since my disenrollment, but that the Marine Corps had finally offered to commission me a captain in the U.S. Marine Corps Reserves and had agreed to a number of other important terms. He told the audience that we were pleased with this resolution, and that I had accepted it. There was a standing ovation. Steve announced that there would be a public commissioning ceremony in Washington, D.C., and then turned the podium over to me. I looked out into the crowd, seeing the smiles on their faces, knowing full well that I could not have made this journey alone.

David has slain Goliath. A grassroots militia armed with nothing more than a belief in justice has vanquished discrimination in the mighty U.S. Marine Corps. In 1989 the Corps said I was a liar and not fit to lead. We fought back. People thought we were crazy. But after five long years filled with fear, frustration, and self-doubt . . . justice has prevailed.

I circled the room, thanking everyone. There were a lot of tears. With each handshake and embrace, I could feel the huge burden being lifted off me. The crowd began to thin. Soon just the inner circle remained. Champagne and crystal flutes appeared out of nowhere. As always, Allicyn had attended to the details that made the difference. Few words were spoken, but after years of struggle, words didn't seem necessary. We all formed a circle, popped the bottle, and toasted the moment.

34

Calling the Shots

SPRING 1994

A WEEK AFTER THE ANNOUNCEMENT, I WAS STILL in a state of disbelief. But reality set in when Marine Corps headquarters called to brief me on the precommissioning process. I reported to the Marine recruiting station on Kapiolani Boulevard, where I had first visited so many years ago. I met Gunnery Sergeant Pagdilao, Gunnery Sergeant Yamashiro, and Corporal Ornellas. They had followed the case. I don't think they realized how much it meant when they asked if they could be in a picture with me in front of the Marine Corps flag. The next day I reported to the Medical Examination Processing Service (MEPS) at the Prince Kuhio Federal Building. I noticed that "Special Physical" was stamped on my chart.

"You have been through enough . . . we're gonna get you through this as smoothly as possible," said the examining physician.

After so many years of feeling like a second-class citizen, I savored the special treatment. I spent the next few hours undergoing a battery of tests. After all that I had gone through, I couldn't help but worry about the unimaginable: flunking the medical. Two anxious days later I returned, and Gunny Yamashiro gave me the news: I had PASSED.

There were just a few final administrative matters. He opened his file cabinet and started going through it. Then he made a telephone call. He went back to the cabinet, and began quickly looking through it again. The examining physician came into the gunny's office, looked at me, and left without a word. They had lost my folder! By now the gunny was frantically rummaging through his desk. I sat

224 there calmly. It was nice to have someone else in the hot seat. Moments later the doctor rushed back in, clutching my folder. The commanding officer had apparently locked it in his safe.

"All we need to do now is lose your physical," he muttered as he walked out.

A week later I was back in Washington. As I took a taxi to Marine Corps headquarters, I felt exhilarated. The OCS standing operating procedures now had provisions that specifically prohibited the use of words or gestures that highlight a candidate's race. The quality management board had sounded the alarm that the Corps needed to improve its efforts to procure, promote, and retain minority officers. In the years after my commissioning, the equal opportunity program implemented a computer database that would track all formal complaints of discrimination, as well as a website that would list equal opportunity policy and regulations. At Quantico, OCS staff would be given ethnic sensitivity training. I would later be contacted by a company commander at OCS, inviting me to speak to his staff about discrimination.

Of course, much remains to be done. The Marine Corps must protect a candidate's constitutional right to due process by providing written notice of his right to file a complaint up the chain of command, or to the NDRB/BCNR. The problem is that the concept that a candidate still has rights is easily lost in the intense atmosphere of OCS. It is not surprising, whether intentionally or by accident, that such written notices over the years have not been given. It is my belief that many legitimate complaints have not been filed because candidates were simply unaware of their rights.

Most important, the Marine Corps must reform an

administrative system that is unable to provide adequate relief for an aggrieved OCS candidate. I had requested the correction of my record, reinstatement, back pay, benefits, and training. The NDRB denied relief because it lacked authority. As stated in their decision, "The ability to grant the applicant the redress he seeks may well rest in the char- **225** ter of another Federal Agency, but it is not within the Naval Discharge Review Board." The BCNR denied relief because evidence submitted was "insufficient to establish the existence of probable material error or injustice warranting relief." The apparent reason for the insufficiency stemmed from the fact that according to the board, my OCS records were not part of my "Official Military Personnel File." How can a candidate make his case, if the very records that he is challenging cannot be reviewed by the BCNR? It became clear that an OCS candidate will find himself in legal limbo: not fully protected by the law, either civilian or military. Marine Corps headquarters denied relief because it did not have the authority, even after an unlawful disenrollment, to provide a retroactive commission. Not surprisingly, Secretary Pang finally intervened, and acknowledged that he had taken extraordinary action because of the "absence of any meaningful alternative remedies."

Finally, relief must not only be adequate, but timely. The Marine Corps must implement a timeline for the investigation and adjudication of complaints. In my case, they were able to drag out the process for five years. It would take an additional three years to fully exhaust my administrative remedies. Time was my biggest enemy. With each passing year, any remedy to undo the harm, even assuming that it was fair and complete, would be increasingly meaningless. In plain terms, what's the practical benefit to the aggrieved candidate if the resolution comes years after his colleagues have graduated from OCS?

After the commissioning, we would continue the legal struggle. We would resubmit our petitions with the

NDRB/BCNR, and later, file a lawsuit in federal court. In 1997, three years after my commissioning, Assistant Secretary of the Navy Bernard Rostker finally addressed an important request. He vetoed the final recommendation of the BCNR, and ordered the Marine Corps to provide service credit by backdating my commissioning to the day that I had been unlawfully disenrolled: April 14, 1989.

But with regard to reforming the system, it would be a tough road. As I had been told years earlier, the federal courts show great deference to the military. But Steve reminded the legal team, "This entire case has been a long shot." Win or lose, we knew that our legal arguments would have to be made, and hopefully, someday, there would be change.

That day, I had a meeting with the Marine Corps to discuss the commissioning ceremony. As I walked down the corridors, a tall, leather-faced colonel came out of his office.

"You're Yamashita, aren't you?"

I was a bit startled. He extended his hand, and I shook it.

"Welcome aboard, Marine," he said with a smile.

Lieutenant Colonel Peal was in charge of coordinating the commissioning. He was waiting for me at the end of the hall. I was not surprised that a black officer was given this assignment. It allowed the Corps to prominently display a minority, and partially insulate itself from any charges of unfairness in handling the ceremony.

Unlike the white officer moments earlier, Peal was formal and distant. There were no congratulations, no small talk. His condescending attitude and cold demeanor reminded me of Captain Garcia. At an earlier time, my mind would have been racing to decipher his personal resentments and motivations. But at that moment, it didn't matter, and I didn't care.

Peal escorted me to a room where twelve white officers, representing different sections involved in my commissioning, were already seated around a table. I couldn't help but recall how it reminded me of being surrounded by Colonel

226

Reinke, Major Winter, and Lieutenant Eshelman at the final battalion review board. But that was a long time ago. This time I would be calling the shots.

Among them was Captain Keating, the officer selection officer (OSO) who had been assigned to me. They briefed me on all aspects of the commissioning process: legal, public affairs, reserves, and administrative. Peal then suggested that the ceremony be held the following week in the basement of Marine headquarters, and that Captain Keating give the commissioning oath. They wanted this thing over and done with. I looked around the table.

"Listen, we all know this is no ordinary commissioning. I need to send invitations to my supporters, public officials, media . . . we will need time to prepare for a proper ceremony."

Peal's face tightened. I emphasized that it was in everyone's interest to do a good job. A proper ceremony couldn't be slapped together. He reluctantly concurred, and asked who I wanted to give the commissioning oath.

"I was thinking of the commandant of the Marine Corps," I said matter-of-factly.

Peal had had enough.

"That is not standing operating procedure!" he said firmly as he stood up from his chair.

I wanted to avoid a direct confrontation.

"Listen, I'll write a letter of request, and if he can't attend then I'd be more than willing to have Captain Keating perform the ceremony," I said calmly.

As the meeting broke up, a tall major shook my hand and wished me luck. Peal left without a word. I did write to the commandant of the Marine Corps requesting that he perform the ceremony, but received a polite refusal. So Captain Keating ended up performing the ceremony, but not the following week, nor at Marine Corps headquarters.

35

"The Struggle Goes On"

MARCH 1994

THE COMMISSIONING CEREMONY WOULD BE HELD on March 18, 1994. As always, nothing had been left to chance. We calculated that Congress would still be in session, and that the worst of winter would be over. Bill and I criss-crossed Washington searching for the perfect location: Marine barracks? Capitol Hill? National Press Club? Iwo Jima memorial? Pentagon? Over lunch we discussed the pros and cons of each location. We finally settled on the House Armed Services Committee Room because it would be convenient for senators, members of Congress, and the media.

The invitations were printed, complete with the Marine Corps logo. Steve would be the master of ceremonies. The speakers would be Randy Senzaki, executive director, national JACL; Stuart Ishimaru, U.S. Civil Rights Commission; Congressman Norman Mineta of California; and members of Hawaii's congressional delegation—Senator Daniel Akaka, Congressman Neil Abercrombie, and Congresswoman Patsy Mink; and Assistant Secretary of the Navy Frederick K. Y. Pang.

Senator Inouye would be conspicuously absent. We had invited him, but he declined. It was a disappointment, but not a surprise. After all, I had rejected the initial offer he had worked out with the Marine Corps. As he had told me, it was like a "slap to the commandant's face." In the end he did what he had to do. And so did I. It was as simple as that. Although he would not be at the commissioning, the fact remained that I owed him a debt of gratitude I could never repay. His backroom political muscle secured my age waiver, which allowed me to attend OCS and was critical to my ultimate commissioning.

Things were coming together. First, I had to get my uniform fitted in Quantico. Driving back was sweet vindication. Unlike the last time I had visited, early in the case, I began to feel a sense of espirit de corps. Since the commissioning announcement, in airports, restaurants, and hotel lobbies, countless active duty Marines had taken the time to congratulate me. Regardless of the official Marine Corps' sentiment on my commissioning, it gave me great hope that there were Marines in the fleet who were troubled by what had happened and shared our pride in the accomplishment.

Past the security post, across the train tracks, and into the town. I parked right in front of the Marine shop near Quantico Pizza. They were expecting me. The sales rep was an attractive young woman with a friendly smile.

"Hey, Wong!" she yelled.

My body froze. Three Chinese tailors came running out from the back of the shop. There was a moment of hesitation, but soon they surrounded me, and began taking my measurements. After five minutes, one of them finally looked up.

"You Japanee?"

After all I had been through, I had to chuckle.

"Yes," I said with a grin.

He smiled and went back to work.

Night after night, I wrote personal notes of thanks on hundreds of invitations. I sent a dozen roses to Jennifer. But I should have sent two dozen. Behind the scenes, she had been crucial to the case. In the end we sent a thousand invitations, but expected about 150 people to attend. There would be a number of people coming from out of town. The inner circle, Margaret and her family, Mother and Pop, and even my high school friend, Oren Iwanaga. Pop was recovering from surgery, but nothing could stop him from making the trip. My brother Allen was flying in from Denver. Judge Miho was extending a trip to the East Coast so that he and his wife could be there.

Already I was receiving congratulatory notes from across the country and the world. They came from friends, supporters, and total strangers. One special card was from Carol Kawamura. She had moved on with her life, but from afar had followed the case. She wrote about how proud she was of me and the accomplishment. Looking at that letter, and the boxes of correspondence, I knew that I had been blessed.

The day before the commissioning was hectic. Steve and his assistant, Lisa Altieri, who had volunteered to help with the commissioning, met me at the Boston House at 7 A.M. Smoking a cigarette, he reported that the weather forecast predicted snow within the next 24 hours. I shook my head, envisioning a snowstorm that would undo weeks of preparation. We walked over to ABC News for a "Good Morning America" interview, then to a nearby hotel for breakfast before grabbing a taxi to the House Armed Service Committee Room. Steve needed to see the room he would be working in. We met Mike Slackman of Abercrombie's office. Then Steve rushed off to prepare.

That afternoon I was inundated with calls from the press. I finalized the media and VIP list and faxed it over to Marine Corps headquarters. I got a haircut. I then raced to the Holiday Inn, where the inner circle was gathered in a booth at the hotel bar.

"Bruce, go home and sleep. Leave the rest to us," said Bill.

My eyes bloodshot, I got up from the table. Bill, Steve, Clayton, Ernie, and Allicyn remained seated. I owed them all so much.

"Well, we started this thing; let's go finish it. Thanks for everything," I said in a quiet voice.

Back at the Boston House, I went over my speech one last time. As I sat there, I reflected on the case. Even with its imperfections, it seemed to meet the steps for an acceptable resolution that we had laid out from the beginning: acknowledgment, apology, and remedy. Of course, the Marine Corps was still avoiding the word "discrimination" in any of their statements. Instead, they used euphemisms such as "racially insensitive treatment." Moreover, I still had doubts about the sincerity of their apology. Did they offer it with true regret? Or was it just lip service to get the media and politicians off their backs? At the commissioning, other than the handful with official duties, none of the Marine Corps brass would be in attendance. Finally, the remedy was far from complete: no back pay, no service credit, no training.

And the fact remained that I would never be a JAG officer and serve on active duty. In the beginning, I had thought that if I fought hard enough, and believed long enough, that everything would turn out right. I believed that ultimately I would live out the images in that colorful recruitment brochure that I had read so many years ago. But I would learn that although justice would be done, it could not turn back the clock. It could not unring the bell. The cold reality was that my dream to serve died with the slam of Colonel Reinke's gavel.

But as imperfect as the resolution was, the principle had been won. The Marine Corps had acknowledged that laws had been broken, apologized, accounted for the years that had passed by commissioning me to the rank of captain, and conceded that the racial remarks may have tainted the evaluations. Moreover, it acknowledged that it had deficiencies with regard to procuring, promoting, and retaining minority officers, and that its affirmative action program was the weakest of all branches of the service. Finally, it had made concrete changes to the SOP to ensure that what happened at the 140th OCS would never happen again.

I realized the importance of forgiveness, not just toward

the Marine Corps, but toward the individuals involved. I needed to go beyond mere resolution to reconciliation. I needed to build bridges, not walls. On this day, I was filled with only goodwill. Some might argue that without a sincere apology and total reparations, the Marine Corps and those involved didn't deserve forgiveness. But forgiveness can be unilateral. For I knew that without it, I might forever limit my view of America to the prism of race. Without it, I might forever be blind to the full potential of America's greatness. Without forgiveness, I could not heal my wounds and start anew.

That night I appreciated more than ever that the individual must choose his battles wisely. He must distinguish between wrongs that merely insult his ego, and wrongs that go to the heart of who he is. A protracted struggle cannot be sustained by being 100 percent on the job; there must be passion fueled by a lofty goal. As my eyes began getting heavy, I knew that I had chosen wisely. This had been a battle that had to be fought. But the price of victory had been high. As others had raced ahead in their careers, I had been mired in a never-ending detour. I had no job; I was in debt; I was exhausted. The next few years would be spent picking up the pieces of my life.

I didn't know it at the time, but ironically my commissioning would coincide with the rise of a conservative tide that would exert its influence for years. The country would witness a backlash against ethnic and religious minorities, women, gays, welfare recipients, and immigrants. Despite the reforms implemented by the Marine Corps, new and disturbing OCS statistics, ending in the year 2001, would reveal that the dropout rate for minority candidates continues to be much higher than that for whites. The attack on the World Trade Center and the Pentagon would further shift the political landscape. More than ever, there would be a need to be vigilant. More than ever, there would be a need to measure our greatness not just by racing ahead, but by reaching back to the powerless and those most vulnerable among us. More than ever, there would be a need to not only ask the questions, but also question the answers. Although my case was coming to a close, the struggle goes on.

Before I knew it, it was 3 A.M. As I slipped into bed, I saw my Marine uniform hanging in the closet. I couldn't help but get up, and run my fingers over the neatly pressed lapel and gaze at the anchor and globe button. At OCS, it meant the glory of a commissioning on the parade deck. Now it stood for so much more. I remembered Aileen Wood, a Korean American grandmother, who had called me during the struggle to provide words of encouragement. For her, it was a reminder of the humiliation she felt marrying her husband despite antimiscegenation laws on the mainland. Or Sonia Aranza, a young congressional staffer, who came to appreciate even more the hardships and indignities her Filipino parents had endured so that she could have a better life. Or Lester Chang, a Chinese American from New York, who had been kicked out of OCS in 1983. He flew down for the ceremony, and would say later, " I've never met Bruce, but this is like my commissioning, this is my justice." For Katsugo Miho, a nisei who supported the case from the beginning, it was an emotional tribute to those who had been unjustly relocated, and comrades who had fought and died during World War II. For my sister Margaret, it merely represented hope that her two sons would live in a better America.

I fell asleep recalling the final press conference, when I had announced my acceptance of the Marine Corps offer. At the end, Mel Ezer, now retired from the University of Hawaii, had come up and given me a bear hug. He had been a passionate supporter from the beginning. Before I knew it, his body was quivering and he was sobbing. My struggle had become their struggle. My vindication had become their vindication. Our victory had become a reminder to keep hope alive, and that collectively we can make a difference in the world.

36

"Justice Will Triumph!"

MARCH 18, 1994

"GOOD MORNING AND ALOHA. FOR THOSE OF YOU not accustomed to snow, we had it this morning, and in such quantity that by this afternoon it will be gone. In Hawaii, rain symbolizes a blessing from the heavens," began Senator Daniel K. Akaka.

Yes, a blessing. God had to be smiling on me. No, I wasn't dreaming. We were really here in the ornate House Armed Services Committee Room with its high ceiling, flags, and emblems of the five branches of the military. The air was perfumed by the flower and *maile* leis flown in from Hawaii. For wintry Washington, D.C., it provided a colorful reminder of how lucky I was to call Hawaii home.

My family was in the front row. Margaret was there with her husband and two young sons. Pop had made it to the ceremony and would witness the end of my struggle. He had lost weight and much of his strength. His face was scarred from surgery and countless radiation treatments, but I could see how proud he was in his own quiet way. I had won my battle; a few months later he would lose his. My father had lived his life believing in the system. This day represented a contract that had finally been honored. I thanked God for answering my prayers, and allowing him to go in peace.

I stood, ramrod straight, face to face with Captain Keating. I slowly raised my right hand. I could feel the flash

Ernie pinning on my captain's bars, 1994.

of light bulbs on my face. I could hear the network cameras whirring. He spoke, and I repeated after him, the oath:

"I do solemnly swear that I will support and defend the Constitution of the United States against all enemies foreign and domestic. That I will bear true faith and allegiance to the same. That I take this obligation freely without any mental reservation or purpose of evasion. That I will well and faithfully discharge the duties of the office on which I am about to enter, so help me God."

Captain Keating gave me a firm handshake. Ernie did the final honors: he pinned the silver captain's bars on my lapel and collar.

It took a couple of minutes, but at that moment I had no concept of time passing. Captain Keating broke the hushed silence.

"Honored guests, ladies and gentlemen, that concludes this commissioning ceremony. It is my distinct pleasure to introduce to you for the first time, Captain Bruce I. Yamashita."

Chapter 36

The audience rose. The applause was deafening. It triggered a surge of emotion in me that broke through any disbelief I still felt. There, standing before me were representatives from the NAACP, Counsel of La Raza, Mexican American Legal Defense Fund, and the Puerto Rican Coalition, showing that support extended far beyond the Asian American community. A friend from International Christian University in Japan had come down from New York to attend the ceremony. I saw a classmate from law school who had read about the case in the papers. The new front desk clerk at the Boston House, a recent immigrant from Cameroon, had taken the day off to attend. And of course, the JACL inner circle, who had been there for me when I needed them most, were there for me again.

Speaker after speaker lauded the accomplishment. As I sat there I recalled the questions that I had asked so many years ago: What kind of leaders humiliate rather than elevate, destroy rather than build? If that was Marine policy, wasn't that policy wrong? Now I knew the answers to those questions. But my journey to justice had taught me much more. Those who had rallied around the case had shown me the meaning of courage, unselfishness, and unwavering commitment to principle. They had given new definition to my sense of patriotism, and made me a better American. They had taught me that we as Americans are a community of people, and an affront to one is an affront to all.

I looked out at the audience and saw a generation in their twilight, one at the high noon of their promise, and another that was too young to understand. Standing before them this day, looking now into their faces, I was reminded of what had sustained me over the years.

I proudly accept this commissioning in tribute to the generations that have come before me: my grandparents, and your grandparents; my parents, and your parents. I accept this commissioning in tribute to their sacrifices, their indignities, their sweat and their blood. I accept this commissioning in tribute to this great nation: never give up, never lose hope, right is might and justice will triumph!

Index

About the Author

BRUCE I. YAMASHITA is a captain in the Marine Corps Reserves. He lives in Washington, D.C., where he practices criminal and immigration law. He continues to advise those who have been wrongfully discharged from the military.

Production Notes for Yamashita/FIGHTING TRADITION

Cover and interior design, and composition by Bookcomp, Inc.
Text in Sabon and display type in Walbaum.

Printing and binding by The Maple-Vail Book Manufacturing Group.

Printed on 50 lb. Glatfelter Hi Opaque.